PRINCIPALITIES AND POWERS

Other Works of Interest from St. Augustine's Press

James V. Schall, S.J., *The Regensburg Lecture*

James V. Schall, S.J., *Modern Age*

James V. Schall, S.J., *The Classical Moment*

James V. Schall, S.J., *The Sum Total of Human Happiness*

James V. Schall, S.J., *Remembering Belloc*

Marc D. Guerra, ed., *Jesursalem, Athens, and Rome:
Essays in Honor of James V. Schall, S.J.*

Kenneth Baker, S.J., *Jesus Christ – True God and True Man*

Ernest Fortin, A.A., *Christianity and Philosophical Culture
in the Fifth Century*

Servais Pinckaers, O.P., *Morality: The Catholic View*

Rémi Brague, *On the God of the Christians
(and on one or two others)*

Richard Peddicord, O.P., *The Sacred Monster of Thomism:
An Introduction to the Life and Legacy of Garrigou-Lagrange, O.P.*

Josef Pieper and Heinz Raskop, *What Catholics Believe*

Josef Pieper, *Happiness and Contemplation*

Peter Geach, *God and the Soul*

Gabriel Marcel, *Man against Mass Society*

Dietrich von Hildebrand, *The Heart*

Robert Hugh Benson, *Lord of the World*

Peter Kreeft, *The Philosophy of Jesus*

Peter Kreeft, *Jesus-Shock,*

Philippe Bénéton, *The Kingdom Sufferth Violence:
The Machiavelli / Erasmus / More Correspondence
and Other Unpublished Documents*

H.S. Gerdil, *The Anti-Emile:
Reflections on the Theory and Preactice of Education
against the Principles of Rousseau*

Edward Feser, *The Last Superstition:
A Reflection on the New Atheism*

Roger Kimball, *The Fortunes of Permanence:
Culture and Anarchy in an Age of Amnesia*

PRINCIPALITIES AND POWERS
Spiritual Combat 1942–1943

GEORGE WILLIAM RUTLER

"For our wrestling is not against flesh and blood; but against
principalities and powers, against the rulers of the world of this
darkness, against the spirits of wickedness in the high places."
(Ephesians 6:12)

ST. AUGUSTINE'S PRESS
South Bend, Indiana

Manufactured in the United States of America

1 2 3 4 5 6   19 18 17 16 15 14 13

Library of Congress Cataloging in Publication Data
Rutler, George W. (George William)
Principalities and powers: spiritual combat, 1942–1943 /
George William Rutler.
pages   cm
Includes index.
ISBN 978-1-58731-662-3 (clothbound: alk. paper)
1. World War, 1939–1945 – Religious aspects – Catholic Church.
2. World War, 1939–1945 – Moral and ethical aspects. I. Title.
D810.C6R87 2013
940.53 – dc23   2013008872

∞ The paper used in this publication meets the minimum requirements of
the American National Standard for Information Sciences Permanence of
Paper for Printed Materials, ANSI Z39.481984.

St. Augustine's Press
www.staugustine.net

Table of Contents

Preface

The following chapters trace, in more or less chronological order, events from June 1942 to June 1943, and personalities that shaped and were shaped by them, analyzed especially in terms of their moral and religious significance. There was no particular reason for choosing these months, save for that they were the period covered in the pile of newspapers and journals and radio transcripts left to me by a friend and historian, Monsignor Florence Cohalan, who had lived through both World Wars and kept what he read. The paper invariably was of poor quality due to war rationing, so I thought that it was time to make use of them, or time would lose them.

The Second World War may be the most thoroughly analyzed few years in human history, of breathtaking scope, with myriad upon myriad of complex intertwinings, for that war encompassed everything that makes up a civilization. These chapters may add little general information that is not already known to some, but I may not be accused of self-deception if I think that they bring together some obscure subjects as contemporaries reported them day by day with lively earnestness.

Newspapers and wire services fed then, as they feed now, on each other, but they often quoted correspondences, personal and public, that fall into the category of oral history more than retrospection. By the nature of the publications I have used, they focus primarily on the role of the Catholic Church which, by its catholicity, was as world-wide as the war itself. This aspect of life lived in wartime has frequently been misunderstood in recent years, and has at least as often been misrepresented by polemicists. My interest in ecclesiastics and their communiqués is born of a conviction that the Second World War can rightly be understood and probably only fully appreciated as a holy war fought for multiple and mixed motives, but in its deepest meaning as a campaign against evil by defenders, consciously or obliviously, of the good.

If anything is to be learned from reading old journals, it is how the same moral dilemmas of an old war, in their display of human dignity and the anatomy of cruelty, are background for the same realities in our day. If a war covers the whole earth, its stratagems are the measureless size of each human soul. "For from within out of the heart of men proceed evil thoughts, adulteries, fornications, murders, thefts, covetousness, wickedness, deceit, lasciviousness, an evil eye, blasphemy, pride, foolishness. All these evil things come from within, and defile a man." (Mark 7:21–23) And from there, they proceed to defile a world.

Henry James wrote to Ivan Turgenev words which may not have accomplished their aim of helping his friend's depression: "Life is, in fact, a battle. Evil is insolent and strong; beauty enchanting but rare; goodness very apt to be weak; folly very apt to be defiant; wickedness to carry the day; imbeciles to be in high places, people of sense in small, and mankind generally unhappy. But the world, as it stands, is no illusion, no phantasm, no evil dream of a night; we wake up to it again forever and ever; we can neither forget it nor deny it nor dispense with it." The battle of life fought in the Second World War left no one untouched. Having taken one year of it as a template for the whole conflict, I have tried to highlight figures, some remembered and others neglected, as ciphers for the many ways people behave in difficult circumstances.

My most thorough source was the weekly London journal *The Tablet*. Venerable for having served the Catholic Church since 1840, in its golden years in the twentieth century its writers included Evelyn Waugh, Hilaire Belloc, Alfred Lunn, Robert Speaight, Graham Greene, Christopher Hollis and, with weekly diligence and erudition, Monsignor Ronald Knox. During the war years, generals and parliamentarians added their words, for it was an honorable and influential thing to be approved by its editor, Douglas Woodruff. He had a very remarkable talent for funneling all sorts of diplomatic and ecclesiastical information which must have been the envy of many embassies and chanceries. Sometimes news from the heart of battles and pogroms was vague and uncertain, and there were reported deaths of people who had not died, but in the days before immediate communication, doubly hampered by censorship, the weekly reporting of *The Tablet* and its friendly allies in the community of journalists did an immense service to the war effort and to history.

I lived through only a few months of the war: I was an infant when Roosevelt and Hitler were still alive, and I was baptized on "VJ Sunday" right after the Japanese surrender. I am told that my diaper was changed on a Liberty ship anchored in Port Newark, when my father had just returned from North Africa. So I can claim to have been on a ship in wartime, though in an inferior capacity. What I knew of the war growing up came to me through my father and virtually every adult man I knew, who had fought in it. I do recall the songs, and among them my mother often sang not as idle nostalgia "The White Cliffs of Dover": "The shepherd will tend his sheep. The valley will bloom again. And Jimmy will go to sleep in his own little room again." Writing about the Second World War now is a feeble act of thanks from my generation who were able to sleep in their own little rooms again only because the brightest and best had contended with brave resolve against the darkest and worst.

1. What Feats He Did That Day

No two people are alike, but everyone is part of one long annal which was being lived ages before anyone was able to write it down. History is mankind's collective biography. One school of historians makes a plausible case for understanding history as nothing but biography. That certainly is a more interesting approach than economic or political history, and one would be hard pressed to imagine economics without real people selling goods, or politics without real people selling themselves.

As a boy, I'd spend rainy afternoons in my grandmother's basement, reading bound volumes of *Life* magazine back to its first issue from November 23, 1936, which featured items about a one-legged mountain climber and Helen Hayes. The second issue included paintings by Adolf Hitler and a passing mention of his deal to supply machinery to Japan. The volumes stopped at the end of 1943. By then, all my uncles who collected the magazines had enlisted and were in some of the war scenes that readers at home only saw in photographs or on the weekly "News of the World" segments in the movie theaters. From then on, history to me was personal, whether reported by Herodotus or Henry Luce. For my grandmother, the Second World War was just the second barrage of the Great War in which her two brothers had been killed within days of each other in the Ypres Salient, and which was not supposed to have a sequel.

A venerable priest and historian whom I knew well did not leave his chapter of history without leaving me a cache of weekly church journals and newspaper reports from 1942 and 1943, which were among the most chaotic days in the biography of man. They began with the Japanese invasion of the Philippines and the simultaneous German assault on North Africa. The "Final Solution" to the "Jewish question" was plotted at Grossen Wannsee, MacArthur left Corregidor, the Bataan Death March began, Laval declared Vichy a German ally, the "Baedeker blitz" revived the 1940 blitzes of the Battle of Britain but this time it was pure revenge ("Vergeltungsangriffe") for the bombing of Lübeck, and its toll was the despoiling of cathedral and abbey towns with no strategic advantage. German submarines tried to sabotage Long Island and New York City (causing my mother and some lady friends to join an ambulance brigade in prudent anticipation of an invasion of New Jersey), the U.S.-Soviet lend-lease agreement was signed, the Allied convoys to Murmansk and Archangel were launched (with personnel including my father), the Germans attacked Stalingrad, the Australians advanced on El Alamein, and the first nuclear chain reaction was set off on a squash court at the University of Chicago.

Of immediate interest to my clerical eyes in these dusty cuttings are the transcripts of Vatican Radio broadcasts, the sermons of bishops in beleaguered countries, papal messages to the conflicted nations, and the obituaries of lay people who had no time to think of themselves as heroes. Those years had more glaring villains and shining saints than almost any portion of the human saga. Reading and reviewing those papers gave me a chance to regress to my boyhood in Grandma's house, where she kept a framed copy of the Canadian John McCrae's poem "In Flanders Fields" which I was required to memorize, with its last lines: "If ye break faith with us who die, We shall not sleep, though poppies grow, In Flanders fields."

On July 18, 2009, Henry Allingham died in England at the age of 113, the oldest living man and the senior veteran of the First World War. He saw the Battle of Jutland and was too old to serve in World War II. The previous year, Franz Kunstler died at 107, the last to fight in that war for the Central Powers in the army of Austria-Hungary. The very last from those battles to leave this world's regiment died in 2011, both at the age of 110: Frank Buckles of the U.S. Army who died on February 27, and

Claude Choules of the British Royal Navy and then the Australian Royal Navy, who died on May 5. The distance from 1942 back to the end of World War I was no longer than we are from the introduction of the first version of Windows by the Microsoft Corporation. But the common biography of those who were at Thermopylae and Agincourt and Verdun and Pearl Harbor blots out distance altogether, if only we manage to stay human. In every army, and every war, troops hear someone shouting with Henry V as bolster and not bluster: "Old men forget; yet all shall be forgot, But he'll remember, with advantages, What feats he did that day."

Some wars can only be understood in two dimensions, for the contrast between good and evil is in them so ripe that what engaged in them was a combat as spiritual as material. This was clearer to some than to others, and the pragmatists who thought they could compromise with the enemy learned that the foe was more Devil than devilish. Charles de Gaulle, who was thrifty in his praise of men, said of the Pope then: "Pius XII judges everything from a perspective that surpasses human beings, their undertakings and their quarrels . . . Pious, compassionate, political – such does this pontiff and sovereign appear to me because of the respect that he inspires in me." To the chagrin and even outrage of the Vichy government, the Pope had received de Gaulle as head of the new provisional government in June of 1944, even before the liberation of France.

Pius XII keeps speaking in the events that follow in this book, sometimes directly and usually through other voices instructed by him. As a child, Eugenio Maria Giuseppe Giovanni Pacelli was moved when an uncle told him of a missionary who been crucified. He said that he wanted to be a martyr but "without the nails." The man the child became learned that there are different kinds of crucifixions and various sorts of nails, bearing witness to the words of the Prince of the Apostles:

> "Always be ready to give an explanation to anyone who asks you for a reason for your hope, but do it with

gentleness and reverence, keeping your conscience clear, so that, when you are maligned, those who defame your good conduct in Christ may themselves be put to shame. For it is better to suffer for doing good, if that be the will of God, than for doing evil." (1 Pet 3:15–17)

His crucifixion without nails began when the mannerly diplomat met face-to-face with Evil, who has two faces and hides one. Through trials Pacelli learned that the strengths of diplomacy can weaken the apostle, which is why the only one of the Twelve to destroy himself was all diplomat and no apostle at all. Forged in earnestness by Pius XI, who was no friend to subtlety, Pacelli constantly mortified his aesthetic desire to imagine things that should be as if they were.

He was consecrated a bishop on the day the Mother of God first appeared at Fatima in 1917 with her prediction of calamities that came to pass very quickly. He knew that optimism as a wish is not hope as a virtue, and that the spiritual combat is not without paradoxes. While his papal coat of arms showed a dove with an olive branch, he instructed the halberded Swiss Guard during the Nazi occupation of Rome to carry machine guns though he stipulated that they were not to be used. With bags packed should he be dragged away in a tense tradition from Maximinus to Napoleon, he marked the line between bravery and bravado and marshaled prudence to save lives when impetuousness could have cost more. With other eyes focused on the Axis, he already was arranging to contend with a future when the Hammer and Sickle went up the flagpole after the Swastika came down. The Chief Rabbi of Romania said in the exhausted year of 1945: "The Catholic Church saved more Jewish lives during the war than all other churches, religious institutions and rescue organizations put together. Its record stands in startling contrast to the International Red Cross and the Western Democracies. . . ."

The faulty architecture of human history is postwar and prewar at the same time. Pius XII never doubted that, after a hot war, a cold war would be long. Jozsef Cardinal Mindszenty was a symbol of the affliction of a new darkness, and the Pope defended him with an uncompromising zeal that sustained the cardinal in later years when he felt bereft. The Pope was satisfied that tyrants should die and closely followed attempts on the life of Hitler. As an incarnation of the tradition of immutable natural law, he concisely explained capital punishment: "Even in the case of the death penalty the State does not dispose of the individual's right to life. Rather, public authority limits itself to depriving the offender of the good of life in expiation for his guilt, after he, through his crime, deprived himself of his own right to life." On the other hand, in light of his loathing of Communism, his simultaneous impulse of mercy could be startling, as when he twice pleaded for clemency for the convicted spies Julius and Ethel Rosenberg – and, in an unprecedented act, published his appeals to President Eisenhower in *L'Osservatore Romano*.

It is dangerous to play Monday-morning quarterback when taking the measure of how people should have behaved in times of crisis. In the romantic cliché of American Indian lore, you can only know a man if you have walked in his moccasins. With a Pope, this means walking in the Shoes of the Fisherman, and only a Pope can do that. If Pius XII harbored an instinct for nuance and indirect indication, his remained a rare voice in a world of immoral silence. Today that silence is deafening in those same institutions that, in those war years, ignored the progress of evil: the universities, the media, and the courts.

No one who lives is sub-human: no baby, however young, and no invalid, however old. To say that in our generation is to indict the academics, journalists, and jurists who stammer when the voice of God calls out, as in Eden: "Where are you?" The tired eyes of the aged barely see what they saw in those terrible years of the 1940s, and young eyes do not see them at all, for they have not been shown what was. There were giants in those days, and there were very small people. Many of the greatest people in wartime were unknown, and the very worst people cannot be forgotten by the best. It is easy to pretend that if we were there then, we would have been worthy of the inscription over the door of a church in Staunton Harold, Leicestershire, which was built by a young nobleman in defiance of the laws of the Protectorate whose policy was to destroy sacred images. Oliver Cromwell demanded that the man finance a ship in punishment for building a church, and put him in the Tower of London where he died in 1656 at the age of 27. At the Restoration, the church was completed by the fiduciary agents for his young son. The inscription reads:

> When all things sacred were throughout ye nation demollisht or profaned Sir Richard Shirley Barronet founded this Church Whose singular praise it is to have done ye best things in ye worst times And hoped them in the most callamitous. The righteous shall be had in everlasting remembrance.

In the lacerating years of the Second World War, of which the following records cover one, the honest self can only say that we would have muddled through the best we could, and that we can still learn from those whose miserable failure at virtue spread misery, and from those whose valor was that of those in every generation who salvage the reputation and repair the dignity of the human race.

2. The Start of a Very Long Summer

Not until of 1942 did the English press receive the transcript of a sermon preached by Cardinal Gerlier, Archbishop of Lyons, the previous December 8, in the basilica of Fourviere. "In truth, all that we have said in the past about the necessity of saving Christian values remains true, . . . The world of the future will be Christian or it will be hell." The report in "La Croix" remarked that "His Eminence declared with emotion that he had rarely been so indignant as when he read recently, in a review which called itself French, some pages where the writer dared to suggest, as a means for rebuilding the world, that Christianity should be 'put to sleep,' and mocked our Divine Saviour, calling him by a term which was intended as a reproach, 'the celebrated Jew'. . . ." The following Easter, the former editor of the Dutch Catholic newspaper "De Unie," banned by the Nazis in 1941, wrote in another Catholic weekly, "De Nieuw Eeuw," that "Christianity is the core of the European spirit and of European culture." In response, the Dutch Nazi weekly, "De Misthoorn," demurred: "Christianity is only a veneer which had given brilliance to European life for some time, but it is also a strait-jacket which has seriously hindered the development of real European and Germanic culture. It is quite unimportant whether or not Christianity takes part in the building of the New Europe. . . Races everywhere in Europe, and especially the Germanic race, with its great creations, will always remain, even if Christianity no longer exists."

It is not difficult to see some anticipation of the verbal dueling between the French and Dutch Christians against the National Socialists in a testimonial quoted by one London editor from a letter of Pope Gregory II to St. Boniface in 722: "Hearing to our great distress, that certain peoples in Germany on the eastern side of the Rhine are wandering in the shadow of death at the instigation of the ancient enemy, and, as it were under the form of the Christian Faith, are still in slavery to the worship of idols, while others who have not as yet any knowledge of God and have not been cleansed by the water of holy baptism, but as pagans, to be likened unto brutes, do not acknowledge their Creator. . . ."

A pastoral letter of Msgr. Sigismund Waitz, prince archbishop of Salzburg, was read in all his churches on October 19, 1941, but only published in London in June 1942. The views of Archbishop Waitz, along with other prominent Austrian clerics such as the Jesuit Rev. Georg Bichimair, were typical of attitudes toward the Jews as "an alien people," as he had said at a Catholic conference in 1925, whose influence had corrupted England, France, Italy and especially the United States, and who were frustrating attempts at political concordats after World War I. He did not share the amiability that made Theodor Cardinal Innitzer a protector and advocate of Christ's "brothers in Judaism." But even the cardinal was strongly reprimanded by Pope Pius XI and Eugenio Cardinal Pacelli for naively welcoming the Anschluss. After Cardinal Innitzer's episcopal palace was ransacked by Hitler Youth in 1939, Archbishop Waitz's own residence was attacked by a Nazi mob shouting for him to be sent to Dachau. His letter, read from the pulpits, said:

> "When I was anointed as a Bishop, the Gospel was placed on my shoulders as God's burden so that I should see that it was preached. We Catholics often have to give way nowadays to outside force. Where earthly matters are concerned we can be patient and silent. Where it concerns our belief, however, there must be no yielding; we must stand firm or die."

Eleven days later, Archbishop Waitz was dead. No physical violence had been done to his person, but at the age of seventy-seven he was overcome by the shock of an evil he had previously underestimated and eventually named for what it was.

On June 7, Msgr. Paul Yu Pin, exiled bishop of Nanking, offered Mass for the Allied cause in Chungking, the Chinese provisional capital. The previous day, he broadcast over the Chinese Central Broadcasting Station to all Catholics in China announcing a National Day of Prayer: "A prayer day is like the stone for David's sling, a simple, foolish, and even scorned way according to many, but which is the most efficacious means of attaining a quick victory and a just and lasting peace." In 1937, the Imperial Japanese Army had offered a $100,000 for his arrest, and thereafter he took refuge in the United States. Having returned to Nanking in 1946, he was expelled by the Communists in 1949. Pope Paul VI created him a cardinal in Rome, where he had been a student at the Angelicum. A youthful-looking figure at age 77 and imposing at 6' 3" height, he died in Rome just before the conclave that elected a successor to the Pope who had given him the red hat.

A June issue of *Feuille*, a small French Protestant newspaper in the unoccupied zone, published a tribute: "The militant Catholics in our country have taken a place which is important and, we do not fear to say, preponderant, at the head of the movement of resistance in which, very often, they have taken the initiative, and of which they remain the inspiration . . . The Catholics have not feared to affirm themselves in the sphere of positive action, and, in spirit of their repugnances, it is they who more often are the soul of the secret associations of resistance, and who publish anti-collaborationist papers. The Protestants of France, in particular, have no right to be ignorant of this immense effort. We shall have to be just towards those who have hastened the hour of material, intellectual and moral liberation, and today we cannot but pay homage to such courageous and radiant spirituality."

On the 13th of June, an SS Standartenführer (Colonel), Paul Blobel, was deputized to destroy evidence of the Nazi "liquidations" in Eastern Europe. Among the SS who prized notoriety, he was esteemed for having enforced the Babi Yar massacres in Kiev under the direction of SS-Obergruppenführer Friedrich Jeckeln. Those slaughters, the principal one of which took place September 29–30, 1941, killing 33,771 Jews, in sum killed somewhere between 100,000 and 150,000 victims: Soviet POWS, Gypsies, and Ukrainian nationalists. Project Sonderaktion 1005 involved the exhumation and cremation of bodies from mass graves and continued to September 1944. Blobel designed structures of iron rails and firewood for expediting the incinerations. He was summoned to the task, having been removed from his command exactly five months earlier for alcoholism. The U.S. Nuremburg Military Tribunal in the Einsatzgruppen Trial sentenced him to death and he was hanged on June 8, 1951, declaring: "May the German people be aware of its enemies!" While exact figures will never be known, he is estimated to have been directly responsible for the deaths of 50,018.

The Italian-occupied zone in France was a refuge for Jews fleeing the Vichy government. But ethnic tensions rattled the cobbled armistice between the Italians and the French. Italian newspapers scorned the bishop of Nice, Msgr. Paul Rémond, as an "Italophobe" for exhorting the Italian boys in his jurisdiction to grow up into "good Frenchmen" and for expressing a wish to be called "*Sa Grandeur*" instead of "*Son Excellence*," since the latter "is a title given in Italy to rogues and cabmen." Between 1942 and 1944, 11,401 Jews in France were deported to death camps, while priests and nuns rescued 12,000. Bishop Rémond designed a subtle and highly effective system for rescuing Jewish children, who were the principal targets of the Vichy racists. Rémond hid children in rectories and convents with elaborately forged documentation. His protocols of charity are described in an account of Greta Herensztat, of Polish Jewish parents who had fled to France. In 1943, at the age of nine, her mother handed her over to "a priest" who was in fact the bishop. Rémond whispered to her: "You are now Ginette Henry. You were born in Orange and your parents are dead. You are going to stay in the convent until we can locate your godparents. Then you will go to live with them as soon as possible. Do you understand? Now repeat your name and your birthplace to me." The archbishop would one day be honored at Yad Vashem as a "Righteous Among the Nations," but he was more pleased that Our Lady of Lourdes, to whom he prayed throughout the war, had healed a 28-year-old woman, Henriette Breseles, of spinal disease on July 3, 1924. On June 4, 1957, having received affidavits from the medical commission, he canonically declared the cure a miracle. Pope Pius XII bestowed on him the personal title of archbishop in 1950, and he died in 1963 just short of his ninetieth birthday.

The London *Tablet* frowned upon the Lord Mayor of Blitz-weary Birmingham for organizing lively summer church services in public parks instead of what he called "mumbled services in cold churches." The editorial comment was equally cold: "The view that worship must have an entertainment value has seldom been so frankly expressed. But American experience has not encouraged those Ministers who have shown a film instead of preaching a sermon. It is the 'reductio ad absurdam' of the foolish and fashionable catering for the modern mind."

A correspondent in Lisbon sends word of the revered English Jesuit Father, C. C. Martindale, a prisoner of war in Denmark for six years: "He sounded much better when he wrote, having had the Last Sacraments about Passion Sunday, and settling down to real angina pectoris. . . . The cold is, I gather, his chief horror. . . . The letter is just like one of his old vivid ones, typed, and of immense length." Father Martindale went on converting souls with wit and stiff upper lip until his death in 1963, close to the death of Archbishop Rémond. Among his many works was a book on the Antichrist, in which he contended, and not as abstract speculation, that Satan is both numbingly banal and inexpressibly insidious.

In the third week of June, various Fascist papers launched new editorial campaigns against the Holy See. These included the "Regime Fascista" and the "Critica Faracosta," whose editor, Giuseppe Bottai, accused the Pope of "culpable neutrality" in the war. Bottai would serve as Minister of Education from 1936 until 1943, during which time he removed all Jewish teachers from the schools and universities throughout Italy, and became Mayor of Rome. In due time, he refurnished his mental household: in July 1943, he joined the unsuccessful coup against Mussolini and later fought for the Allies in the French Foreign Legion.

Against this backdrop, the Vatican's own *L'Osservatore Romano* commented approvingly of the recent trip to the United States by the prime minister of the Polish Government in Exile, General Władysław Sikorski, and hoped that Poland would remain true to her ideals of freedom and would stand by the principles of the Atlantic Charter.

The newspaper of Poles exiled in London, *Wiadomośir Polskie*, prints a prophecy of the naturalist and political activist Count Włodzimierz Dzieduszycki of Lwow written in 1890, nine years before his death:

> "As anything is possible, it may happen that the King of Prussia and the Prussian Junkers will put themselves at the head of a social movement and on its basis establish a new political order. Or, from among the workers there may emerge a dictator who will achieve this after the downfall of the now reigning dynasties. The voice of pessimism will then be hushed for a while and history will witness a final and terrible attempt to realize the German ideal on a new, democratic, foundation. The might of Germany will reach its apogee, individual liberty will shrink in all fields, labour will be intensified, happiness will disappear, and pessimism, returning with a smile of triumph, will proceed to carry out the suicide of a great nation."

3. An Ugly Amount of Success

English Catholics had ample opportunity to ponder the variety of lives in the macabre litany of obituaries which seemed to lengthen with each week of summer. They were of all sorts and conditions, but all of them were part of a long drama of which the present years were being fought so that there might be acts yet to come. There was the death on July 10 of Lieutenant-General Sir George Macdonogh, G.B.E., K.C.B., K.C.M.G. At the age of 77, his life spanned the Second Afghan War, the Zulu War, the Boer War, and two World Wars. As the chief architect of modern military intelligence at the War Office, he suitably "was the author of the Defence of the Realm regulations which, when sanctioned by Parliament, became a household word as 'Dora.' He was a man sparing of speech, who preferred to listen." A Knight of Malta long active in Catholic charities which he funded through his various successful business interests, Sir George was a notable friend of beleaguered Finland, the homeland of his wife.

In contrast to that venerable knight, on July 15, dashing Wing Commander Brendan Eamon Fergus "Paddy" Finucane died at only 21, having won the D.S.O. and D.F.C. with two bars after shooting down 32 German flyers, 26 single-handedly. In March, he had brought down four Focke Wulf Fw 190s and had become so celebrated that models of his Spitfire decorated with shamrocks were sold in British toy shops. His death came one month after he had been made the youngest wing commander in the history of the RAF. "A casual onlooker might be pardoned for thinking him a dare-devil type." But he was a moderate pipe-smoker and almost a teetotaler. A friend writes: "Besides an impression of great vitality and quickness, his face revealed two grand qualities; his absolute straightness and utter cleanness. I shall like to think of him as I saw him the Sunday before he met his death – kneeling down at Mass, saying his beads with complete simplicity." His last flight was an attack on a German army camp in Etaples, France, after which he flew his crippled airplane off the coast. His last words to his crew before crashing into the sea were, "This is it, chaps." One of his uniforms is in the RAF museum in London and his name in inscribed on the monument to "The Few" on the Embankment and on the RAF memorial at Runnymede for those whose remains were not found. A Requiem Mass was sung in Westminster Cathedral on July 29.

The death of Miss Alice Howard, youngest daughter of Sir Henry Howard, the first British Minister to the Holy See, brought back memories of the First World War, when her father, the retired British ambassador to the Netherlands, was appointed in 1914 to congratulate Pope Benedict XV on his election and to press upon him the case for Britain's involvement in the war. Miss Howard had opened a tea shop in her little Cotswold village of Painswick to raise funds for a Catholic chapel and eventually was able to turn a slaughterhouse into a church, which she presented to the diocese. After so many years of work, an air raid destroyed it, but she was able to rebuild it in time for her funeral.

Across the Channel, the Vichy government was trying to elicit clerical support by promulgating measures abrogating the anticlerical laws of 1904. The Carthusians returned to France, and property was restored to the Grande Chartreuse. Dominicans and Jesuits were suspicious, and the archbishop of Carthage, Msgr. Charles-Albert Gounot, warned against the State control of the Church. The Jesuit journal *Cité Nouvelle* said that "neither France nor the Church stands to gain anything from a *'Gouvernement des curés.'*"

For the Allies, the general picture was bleak, and the enemy was attacking in Russia and the Atlantic "hard and with an ugly amount of success." Franco told the new Spanish Cortes that there was "no hope in the liberal-democratic system. The totalitarian system has shown itself to be obviously superior in the military field. In the economic field it is the only system that can save a nation from ruin."

Meanwhile, even the Hungarian premier was obliged formally to regret Axis-backed atrocities against Serbs in Novi Sad on the Serb-Hungarian frontier. This slaughter of a thousand captives would be re-enacted in the 1966 film *Hideg Napok*.

In Yugoslavia, Bishop Alojzije Mišić of Mostar expressed horror at the massacres of Serbs with the complicity of Herzegovinian Franciscans headquartered at Široki Brijeg near Medjugorje, a Ustaše center. Bishop Mišić described hundreds of women and children thrown alive into ravines at Surmanci. Eugene Cardinal Tisserant grimaced: the Franciscans behaved "abominably." And in Greece, in response to the shooting of hostages, the Archbishop Chrysanthos of Athens, who in 1941 had refused to swear in the new quisling government of Georgios Tsolakoglou, put a solemn curse on Gunther Altenburg, the German plenipotentiary. Having resigned his office, Chrysanthos lived in self-imposed confinement and virtual poverty in a small house in Athens. His successor, Archbishop Damaskinos, continued to defy the Nazi demands to round up Jews for forced labor and ordered his people to hide them. In a house directly across the street from his residence, the Princess Alice of Battenberg, mother of Britain's Prince Philip, nearly starving herself, cooperated with Damaskinos in hiding Jews. In September 1943, when Schutzstaffel commander Jürgen Stroop threatened to put Damaskinos before a firing squad, the archbishop replied by recalling the lynching of Patriarch Gregory of Constantinople by the Turks in 1821: "According to the tradition of the Greek Orthodox Church, our prelates are hanged, not shot. Please respect our tradition." Both Chrysanthos and Damaskinos died, honored by their people, in 1949. Princess Alice founded a nursing order of nuns, wore a habit, and died in Buckingham Palace in 1966. In 1988 her remains were buried on the Mount of Olives in Jerusalem.

Jozef-Ernest Cardinal van Roey, Primate of Belgium, castigated Nazi race theory as a materialist contradiction of Catholicism and was ridiculed as obscurantist by the newspapers: "Take, first, the conception of man and of life according to these new ideas. The doctrine of blood and race comes to this: blood is the principle of life – not only of physical, vegetative, sensitive life, but also of spiritual life, of the acts of the will, of the intelligence, and all that is beautiful in man. . . .There are superior races and inferior races, by virtue of their blood, the former being destined to dominate the others. To that purely materialistic doctrine Christian spiritual doctrine stands in direct opposition."

Writing in a July issue of "Commonweal," Wilhelm Spozbacher described the German Civil Administration set up in Luxembourg to make the Grand Duchy "German again." Under the direction of Nazi Gauleiter Gustav Simon, who had a notorious criminal record, even the French language and the term "Grand Duchy" were forbidden and all organizations were incorporated into Nazi organizations. Although membership in the German Racial Movement (Volks-Deutsche Bewegung) and the Hitler Youth (Volks-Jugend) was compulsory for many segments of the population, they met with a considerable degree of passive resistance. The Catholic witness was crippled after the death in the SS prison in Berlin in June, 1941, of the editor of the Catholic daily newspaper, "Luxembourger Wort." In Hohwald, a convent was emptied on two hours' notice and the nuns were left in the street, and, in a night raid, the Benedictine monks of the Abbey of Clervaux were given one hour to leave. The stage was being set in these mid-summer weeks for the formal annexation of Luxembourg to the Third Reich on August 30.

In July, the Vatican Radio broadcast the anti-Nazi pastoral letter of the bishop of Calahorra, Spain, for the first time in German. Public figures in our day who claim to be Catholic but who cast a blind eye to eugenics in return for government appointments and subsidies are bad echoes of figures like the Italian Fascist Roberto Farinacci, who appointed himself mayor of Cremona and, with a kind of semantic acrobatics, proceeded to ridicule the hierarchy as "Pseudo-Catholics." Secular journalists were among the most docile to the new dictators. When the Milanese-Catholic journal *Italia* published a letter of Britain's Arthur Cardinal Hinsley, which spoke of the sufferings of the Poles, Farinacci, who called himself a practicing Catholic, ranted: "Cardinal Hinsley is acting in complete bad faith. . . . As regards Poland, our opinion remains unchanged, whatever the Vatican Radio may say. The People of Poland for many years were corrupted by the sons of Judah." In a speech in the Teatro Linco in Milan, on July 4, Farinacci said: "If one considers calmly the heroic spectacle offered by Europe, one should be filled with pain and anger at the mere thought that people can still discuss whether or not it is permissible to be irreconcilable enemies of the Jews. The true Christian has no need to refer for advice to pseudo-Catholic newspapers, or to seek inspiration from some homily in order to get permission for this purifying and redeeming action. In waging this supreme struggle, we are sure of obeying the injunctions of the Church; we are sure of doing our duty as Christians."

The Catholic press responded, saying that Farinacci had apparently forgotten the official declaration of the Holy Office issued from the Vatican on March 25, 1928: "Moved by the spirit of charity, the Apostolic See has protected the people (of Israel) against unjust persecutions, and since it condemns all jealousy and strife among peoples, it accordingly condemns with all its might the hatred directed against a people which was chosen by God; that particular hatred, in fact, which to-day commonly goes by the name of anti-Semitism."

Vatican historians are never likely to let an obscure anniversary pass by unnoticed, and someone in their ranks must have enjoyed especially mentioning on the Vatican Radio's program in Polish for July 21 that it was the four-hundredth anniversary of the Bull "Licet ab Initio," with which Pope Paul III declared that the Roman inquisition would be the supreme tribunal for the whole world. The radio assured the Poles: "The defense of

Divine Truth and Christian principles has ever since been the duty, and indeed the 'ratio essendi,' of the Holy See; which hence always opposes any power which falls into error. It does not concern itself with the popularity or unpopularity of its pronouncements, which are often directed, when the need arises, against the very idols of this world."

On July 16, the deportation of Jews from Paris started. The Battle of Stalingrad began the next day, and on the 24th, the Red Army began to retreat along the Don River after the Germans took Rostov. The First Battle of El Alamein, for all practical purposes, ended on July 26 when General Auchinleck, who had swapped jobs with General Archibald Wavell as Commander in Chief of the Indian Army in order to take over the British Eighth Army in North Africa, failed in his attack against Rommel. "The Auk" and Churchill did not agree on strategy, nor did he get on with his former subordinate, Bernard Montgomery, who was not by nature given to subordination, and Auchinleck returned to India as Commander-in-Chief, highly respected by many governments. He renewed his affinity for North Africa by retiring, after some time in London, to Marrakesh where he lived in comparative obscurity and died in 1981 at the age of 96. Montgomery took over the Eighth Army on August 13, as the Germans were approaching Stalingrad. Six days later British forces made of mostly Canadian troops would be killed or captured by German defenders of Dieppe in France.

On the day of the British defeat in the First Battle of El Alamein, Father Titus Brandsma died in Dachau. Father Brandsma was a Discalced Carmelite priest, professor of philosophy and the history of mysticism at the University of Nijmegen. The year 1942 was the fourth centenary of the death of St. John of the Cross, the central subject of Father Brandsma's scholarly life. He gave his rosary to the Allgemeine SS doctor who administered the injection.

4. Life Goes On

If our present existence were not sufficient proof, the irrefutable platitude that life goes on was evident in August 1942 in England when, coincident with the bombings and lengthening list of war casualties and stricter food rationing, Aloysius Roche published a preview of his study of the Egyptian Desert Fathers, and T. S. Eliot lectured the Classical Association on "The Classics and the Man of Letters." The Lady Abbess of Oulton, the Rt. Rev. Dame Gertrude Beech, marked her golden jubilee in religion, and five churches designed by Pugin celebrated their centenaries. At the same time, government censors revealed the destruction by enemy action of Pugin's church at Handsworth, Birmingham, and damage to St. Chad's Cathedral and the Oratory in Edgbaston. The Birmingham Blitz, begun two years before, would end on St. George's Day, April 23, 1943. On the Feast of the Assumption, Archbishop Peter Amigo carried the Blessed Sacrament in procession around the ruins of St. George's Cathedral in Southwark, London, where Pugin had been the first person to be married after he had built it in 1848, the first Catholic cathedral built in England since the Reformation.

Celebrating the golden jubilee of this priestly ordination on August 1, Cardinal Faulhaber published a pastoral letter on the priesthood as it was suffering under the present regime, to be read in all the churches of the Archdiocese of Munich. The Vatican radio broadcast it in its German program to the wider Reich. "Christ's prophecy, 'Ye shall drain the cup that I have drained,' has been fulfilled in the priests. Just as He Who redeemed mankind had to submit to the most damnable indictments, to the charge even of corrupting the people, so the priest is called upon to share in the Passion of his Master. Time after time he is confronted with the demoniacal principle, 'Strike at the shepherd and the flock will scatter'...At all time has the law of celibacy been slandered, jeered at and dragged into the mire. Priests are said to have transgressed. But no sane person will judge a tree by its windfalls, or the spirit of an army by its deserters . . . No earthly power can force a young man who feels the call to the priesthood to choose another career."

The protocols of life proceeded in Rome, where Pope Pius XII received in audience the Comte de Paris, pretender to the throne of France, who was to be best man at the wedding of the Duke of Bragança, pretender to the throne of Portugal, to the elder sister of Dom Pedro-Gastão de Alcántara d'Orléans-Bragança, pretender to the throne of Brazil. But at the same time real sabers were rattling nearby.

Giuseppi Bottai, the Italian minister for education and editor of the review *Critica Fascista*, wrote in the opaque rotundity that has not ceased being dear to some Italian journalists that Italian Catholics have never followed their bishops blindly, and so they should ignore the Vatican's "insistent propaganda in favour of the principles of natural law and international justice," which contradicted "concrete historical reality" and "encouraged the enemies of the Axis and their insidious egalitarian policy." The Fascists were greatly upset when, in the presence of the Pope and 25,000 worshipers, Carlo Cardinal Salotti preached a sermon in which he attacked the logic of the war and desired "a kingdom of love that will be proof against the errors made in the name of race and nation, a kingdom of liberty which will make tyranny impossible, a kingdom of the spirit which will free men from materialism."

Meanwhile, the Pope personally requested Bishop Francesco Borgongini-Duca, the Apostolic Nuncio to Italy, to visit the Chinese internees, including the Franciscan priest, Father Antonio Tchang, in a concentration camp at Tossicia. The bishop instructed forty-two Chinese converts and received them into the Church. Earlier, Msgr. Borgongini-Duca visited another camp whose Jewish prisoners said that the visit gave them "new courage to go on living." In a letter to the Pope, they addressed Pius XII as a "revered personality who has stood up for the rights of all afflicted and powerless people."

As life went on in Holland, Dr. Anton van Duinkerken, a writer for a Catholic literary magazine for young people, was taken hostage by the Nazis along with the Catholic novelist Dr. Anton Coolen; the leading Catholic intellectual review, *De Nieuwe Eeuw*, kept printing until German soldiers trashed its offices.

In the same weeks of August, the Patriarch of Lisbon, Manuel Cardinal Cerejeira, told the National Council for Catholic Action of Adult Men that Catholics must not oppose democratic ideals "because Christianity was their mother." Cardinal Cerejeira, who had been a friend of Dr. Salazar at the University of Coimbra, believed that Salazar's "moderate dictatorship" should be only "a temporary measure," otherwise "it would be hard to avoid State control of corporations which were planned originally to be free professional and vocational organizations." A Catholic press service said, "Now that the war has clarified the ultimate issues of freedom or slavery, and the values of the English and American democracies have withstood the ordeal, the Cardinal thinks the moment has come to revive democratic ideals in Portugal." Almost ninety when he died in 1977, he outlived Salazar by seven years; and his forty-eight years in the College of Cardinals were surpassed only by Cardinal Prince Henry Stuart's fifty-eight-year-long cardinalate, which began when he was twenty-two.

According to Britain's "Jewish Chronicle," a newspaper founded in 1841, 146 Catholic organizations in Latin America and in Europe, including Italy, had asked the Holy See to intervene in Berlin against the Nazi killings of Jews. It also reported that the Apostolic Nuncio in Germany had already made representations, which were rejected by the Nazi Government as having no bearing on "Internal German policy." The Apostolic Nuncio in France, Msgr. Valerio Valer, formally protested to the

Vichy Government against the imprisonment of Jews. He denounced Pétain's public claim that the Pope supported Vichy's campaign against the Jews. The German government was quick to quote the rejoinder of Laval who "could not be influenced by the Holy See." On August 6, "The New York Times" ran a headline: "Pope is Said to Plead for Jews Listed for Removal from France." According to "La Marseillaise," the Vichy Minister of Information, René Jollivet, on August 8 forbade the Press "to mention the démarche made to the Head of State by Msgr. Valeri, in the name of the Pope, in favor of the Jews." Three weeks later, "The New York Times" had another headline: "Vichy Seizes Jews; Pope Pius Ignored."

The "Schweizer Kirchezeitung" reported that the archbishops and bishops of Occupied France held a conference in those torrid August days to protest against the "Vel d'Hiv" roundup of Jews for deportation to camps in Eastern Europe which had been launched on July 16 in the unoccupied zone, reaching a high intensity early September. French police had confined 13,152 Jews at the Velodrome d'Hiver, the enclosed winter arena used for bicycle races and such, for transportation to Auschwitz by way of Drancy. As the French media censored their appeals to Marshal Pétain, they arranged for their message to be passed around the nation from mouth to mouth: "It is in the name of humanity and in the name of Christian principles that we raise our voice to protest in favour of the rights of the human person." The bishop of Montauban wrote in a Pastoral Letter: "In Paris, Jews by the tens of thousands are being treated in the most barbarous and savage manner. . . . May God console and fortify those who are so abominably persecuted, and give men a true and lasting peace based on justice and charity."

The "Jewish Chronicle" editorialized that "Catholic priests have taken a leading part in hiding hunted Jews and sheltering the children of those who are under arrest or who have been deported to Germany. Laval has now ordered the arrest of all Catholic priests in whose presbyteries hidden Jewish children are found." As archbishop of Lyons and primate of France,

Pierre-Marie Cardinal Gerlier threatened to excommunicate anyone who bought property unjustly seized from Jewish families, and instructed Catholics to hide the children of Jews who had were in French concentration camps or who had been deported to Germany.

Hundreds of priests were arrested, including eight Jesuit Fathers and ten Dominicans, on the island of Saint-Marguerite, charged with "Gaulliste activities." Cardinal Gerlier would live to the age of eighty. In 1981, like the Bishop of Nice, Yad Vashem gave him posthumously the title "Righteous Among the Nations."

Through the end of July and beginning of August, Signor Farinacci continued his disputes with the Catholic newspaper of Milan, "Italia." He objected to anti-Fascist pamphlets distributed among the students of the Catholic University of Milan. "Italia" replied that Farinacci's attacks were "launched not only against Catholic newspapers, but also against the Cardinals, the Vatican, and the Holy See (and therefore against the Pope)." Farinacci's diatribes were like a comic paper that could be read for "buon umore." "Experience of two wars has taught many things, and this among others: that there is always someone who will lend himself to the vile business of badgering ('tenere sulla corda') Catholics, clergy, and the Pope himself for propaganda reasons." It was the description of him as a unintentional comedian that puffed Farinacci's rhetoric up to his fullest bombast. As for any pious obligation to follow the Vatican and the Vatican Press: "This is a colossal mistake. In the first place, for reasons which we might describe as constitutional, the Church is universal, international, and supernational. We, on the other hand, are fiercely dutifully, and exclusively Italian Catholics – that is, Fascist Catholics. Undoubtedly, we could not agree with the Vatican Wireless broadcasts of sympathy for Jewish Poland; the telegram sent to the Protestant Queen Wilhelmina; the considerable contribution made to the Holy See a few years ago by the Jews; the failure to take up a position against Russia; the failure to protest against and condemn the contaminating religious unions between Jews, Protestants and Catholics in the United States and great Britain; the appointment of Jews to posts in the Vatican City, almost in defiance of our anti-Semitic (and therefore Catholic) policy."

The Vatican sent word to the Polish Government in London that the Holy See had recently made several interventions to the German government about the terrible treatment of the Poles in prisons and in concentration camps. Hitler responded by expressly refusing to release Polish bishops and priests in custody. In preparation for the Feast of the Assumption, on August 15, Pope Pius XII received in audience the Chapter of the Sisters of the Holy Family of Nazareth, whose Polish foundress in 1875 was Franciszka Siedliska. His words were unusually emotive: "Tell everybody the Pope loves Poland; he who says otherwise is lying." He also gave the entire Polish nation the Apostolic blessing in a letter sent to Cardinal Hlond, exiled in Lourdes: "By holding firmly to their Catholic faith – the religion of their ancestors – the Poles have achieved new and even greater strength than ever before. Thanks to their faith they have risen, in spite of the present catastrophe, to acts of splendid heroism." Given the emergency conditions, the Pope on May 16 had granted "for the duration of the war a plenary Indulgence for all living in Polish territories who, at the point of death and being unable to confess or communicate, invoke even mentally the Holy Name of Jesus with sorrow for their sins, and accept their death with resignation."

On the Vigil of the Assumption, the Salesians announced that 120 members of their Order had been put to death by the Gestapo in Poland. It was the first anniversary of the death of Father Maximilian Kolbe at Auschwitz, by an injection of carbolic acid. Newspapers had little or no information of many of the martyrdoms and they also received reports that turned out to be false, such as the supposed death at Auschwitz of the Rev. Jan Piwowarczyk, rector of the Theological Seminary at Krakow. He was unharmed and received a new class of seminarians in Autumn of 1942. One of the new aspirants for Holy Orders was

Karol Wojtyła. As Pope John Paul II, he would canonize Kolbe in 1982, and beatify the 31-year-old Salesian Father Joseph Kowalski, who was killed in Auschwitz on July 4, 1942, the day the first air missions by the U.S. Air Force began in Europe. He died after being tortured for refusing to trample on a rosary. The previous week, another Salesian, Father František Miska, died in Dachau. On May 12, 2011, the investigative process for his beatification was formally completed.

On the same Vigil of the Assumption, a message was broadcast in English by the Vatican Radio saying: "It is necessary to increase the volume of the present Vatican stations very considerably, especially as they cannot be too well received even in Italy. A new medium-wave station is required, so that the Holy Father's voice can be heard in all parts of the globe." Americans were reminded of the war's global reach when a Japanese air attack on August 28 started a forest fire in Oregon.

On August 15, the "Compagnons de France," a youth group sympathetic to the Resistance, carried in procession to Le Puy a statue of Notre Dame de Strasbourg, in a not-subtle rejection of German governance of Alsace and Lorraine. When the local officials of Mulhouse were constrained to rename some street for Adolf Hitler, they obliged, but the street they selected was the Rue du Sauvage. Not a youth but an elderly Breton woman near Lorient, bent under a load of firewood in an area of heavy Allied bombardment, said, "I lost two sons in 1914, and a grandson in this war. I have two others prisoners, but I will face the loss of them if it is necessary for the life of France and so that we and our Allies win the war." The youthful procession had so deeply exercised the Nazis that the September 1 issue of the "Kölnische Zeitung" resented that it had "clearly shown the chauvinistic policy of the Catholic Church." The particularly grating attendance of the Bishop of Metz "opened up the whole question of the French claims in Alsace and Lorraine."

There had been speculation in July that Franco would restore the Spanish monarchy, though it was assumed that Don Juan would be king. This was encouraged by the Allies, for his mother was English and he had been educated with the English navy. Of the European kings, only two were collaborators with Hitler: King Boris of Bulgaria and the feckless Italian King Umberto. Leopold of the Belgians was a determined resister and prisoner of war, and the Allies had the support of the kings of Yugoslavia, Greece and Norway, and Queen Wilhelmina of the Netherlands, for whom Hitler was "the arch-enemy of mankind," was held in particular affection. She reluctantly accepted King George VI's offer of refuge in England, but only after having shown remarkable bravery under Luftwaffe attacks. Her wealth as the richest woman in the world enabled her to support many war efforts out-of-pocket. Her broadcasts to her homeland were listened to attentively by her people. On August 5, 1942 she was the first queen to address the joint houses of Congress. A solemn High Mass was celebrated in the Farm Street Church, London, on her sixty-second birthday, though the Queen was not a Catholic, and a Dutch priest who had recently escaped to England preached the sermon.

Hitler disdained monarchies as representing a nationalist sentiment inimical to the mythic universalism of his Reich. So he did not regret the evaporation of the royal houses of Bavaria and the smaller German states. As an anxious bourgeois, Hitler shook his fist against the protocols and precepts of the old order. He especially resented the Habsburgs and joined a Bavarian division across the German border in the First World War. He did request a meeting with the young Archduke Otto, son of Emperor Karl of Austria-Hungary under whose rule he had been born. The Archduke, heir to the emperor whom Pope John Paul II beatified, said with the heroic humility that dispenses with modesty, "He is not worthy." Hitler sentenced the Archduke Otto to death in absentia. The British press generally thought that King Christian of Denmark, stolid enough in refusing to consent to National Socialism, was too passive during the occupation of his country. The Danes, however, were moved by his daily rides on a horse through the streets of Copenhagen without any security, as a sign of national defiance. At one point, his coldness to Hitler became the efficient cause for the recall of the German ambassador. In contrast, his brother, King Haakon of Norway, was admired for preferring exile rather than surrender his sovereignty. At the end of the war, his return from London was accorded the welcome of a hero.

Prince George, Duke of Kent, the younger brother of King George VI, died as an RAF Air Commodore in a plane crash in Caithness, Scotland on his way to Iceland on August 25. His death tied the royal family ever closer to their people, and this much-liked prince ended his louche and complicated existence like the Thane of Cawdor – "Nothing in his life became him like the leaving it."

5. Passing through a Severe Calvary

Marking the end of the third year of war, Italy seemed fated to lose, whichever side won. Germany began to view Mussolini as Churchill described the relationship, "a lackey and a serf, the merest utensil of his master's will." Italian aspirations for "*spazio vitale*" were not mentioned when Joseph Goebbels was in Venice to open an international cinema exhibition, and the propaganda minister, Alessandro Pavolini, hunkered down very much in his big shadow. The Italian Fascists began to sense that Vichy might replace Rome as the second capital of Berlin's New Order.

If France had not been scrupulous in respecting its traditional honorific as "the Eldest Daughter of the Church," the Holy See regarded its history and vicissitudes as conferring a special gravity upon what the Apostolic Nuncio said and did there. Going back to the accords of the Congress of Vienna in 1815, the Apostolic Nuncio was ex officio dean of the diplomatic corps. At the last annual diplomatic reception on New Year's Day at Vichy, Msgr. Valerio Valeri had spoken against the government's anti-Semitism. The outrage of Laval had simmered over the months, finally bursting when the Nuncio had spoken again in the summer about the deportations.

A broadcaster on the collaborationist Radio Paris on September 2 exploded: "An apparently unassuming person of whom the general public is only accustomed to hear on New Year's Day went to Vichy to protest against the treatment rightly meted out to foreign Jews. It was not the chief Rabbi who made the protest, but the kindly discretion of the step did not prevent the whole world from learning of it at once. Jews by birth, synthetic Jews, all published it abroad that one of the highest moral authorities had stigmatized, and rightly so, the French Government's treatment of Israel. Let us not hesitate to say that the Envoy of the Church should have abstained from such action. His gesture amply justified those who maintain that this temporal act of his is extremely perfidious at the present moment, since it causes the faithful to obstruct the National Revolution. It is permissible to ask why certain Vatican cliques, usually so circumspect, fly up in the air every time it is a question of the descendants of Christ's murderers . . . True, it is not only today that we observe this special affection of a section of the Catholic Church for Jews, Freemasons and Democracy. It should be realized how partisan actions brand those who take them. There are political screens, behind which can be seen the tip of a hooked nose, which try to deceive the mass of French Catholics who have not yet confused their religious faith with their political opinions. . . ." On September 4, "The New York Times" described the consequences: "Laval Spurns Pope – 25,000 Jews In France Arrested for Deportation."

Given the many public statements of Valeri, three times in August 1942 alone, history is ill-served by later commentaries that depict him as a "collaborationist" lumped together with the nearly two dozen French bishops who were guilty of collaboration and were removed from office by Valeri's successor in France, Msgr. Angelo Giuseppe Roncalli, at the direction of Pius XII. Valeri had the difficult, if not impossible, task of representing the Holy See to a France divided politically and strategically. Once the French government was moved from Paris to Vichy, the Roman Curia was divided over whether its Nuncio (Valeri had been appointed in 1939) should be recalled and replaced with a chargé d'affaires in the Paris nunciature. Valeri remained, and performed boldly, if without result, as a legate embodying the Pope's contempt for Vichy's posturing. At the Liberation in 1944, de Gaulle requested the replacement of Valeri, not for any malignant sentiments on the part of the Nuncio, but to make clear the break with the past, and his own evident conviction that there should have been no Nuncio to the government of

Pétain. De Gaulle would not allow any imputation of senility to excuse Petain's contemptible association with Laval The pathetic old general may have been toothless in more ways than one, but Laval wielded a baton so heavy and blunt that he shocked even some of the Nazi overlords. Msgr. Roncalli was appointed Nuncio to Paris on December 19, 1944, in time to represent the the diplomatic corps on New Year's Day as doyen, as Valeri had done to the chagrin of Vichy. De Gaulle received Valeri the next day with friendly expressions of gratitude for his services to the Free French, and bestowed on him the Legion d'Honneur. De Gaulle also showed his satisfaction by appointing as minister to the Holy See Jacques Maritain, the theologian agreeable to Pius XII and "maestro" in the estimation of Msgr. Montini, "substitute for ordinary affairs" under the Secretary of State, Luigi Cardinal Maglione. If there was any collaboration in Valeri, it was with the opposite team, and, in the first week of October following his summer crisis with Vichy, he followed his private audience with the Pope with a private conversation with Roosevelt's personal representative to the Holy See, Myron Taylor. In 1953, Pius XII made Valeri Prefect of the Sacred Congregation for Religious and created him a cardinal.

Early in September, Cardinal Gerlier hid nine Jewish children. Adolf Eichmann ordered the Prefect of Lyons to seize them four days later. Finding that they were no longer in the Cardinal's residence, the Prefect demanded to know where they had been taken. Gerlier's reply was succinct and deliberately void of the tact he would have used had he been addressing a gentleman: "Monsieur le Prefet, I would not consider myself worthy to be the Archbishop of Lyons if I complied with your request. Good day."

One of Gerlier's aides, Father Pierre Chaillet, S.J., was detained in the small town of Privas, an old Huguenot center 70 miles outside Lyons, once nearly destroyed by Richelieu. He was able to hide about 1,000 Jews, mostly children, in area monasteries, and even smuggle them to Switzerland and Spain. His guilelessness and disguise as a local parish priest enabled him to persuade the Gestapo to release him more than once. Throughout the war he remained active in the Resistance and in 1972 at Yad Vashem, the Jewish people inscribed him as one of the "Righteous among the Nations." At the time of Chaillet's first arrest, Pierre Laval, as Prime Minister, told foreign correspondents in Vichy: "Nobody and nothing can sway me from my determination to rid France of foreign Jews. Cardinals and bishops have intervened, but everyone is a master of his own trade. They handle religion. I handle government."

On September 4, the day after the Battle of Stalingrad began with the Red Army conscripting even civilian boys and elderly men, Pétain created the Service du Travail Obligatoire (STO), a forced labor program, which became a chief moral issue for the Church. The Vichy government also increased efforts to fabricate a preposterous "Celtic Gaul" racialist mythology with an exaltation of *"le plateau druidique"* represented by poster images of a druidical oak-leaf sprouting out of the heart of France. At Gergovia, a contrived celebration of the defeat of the Romans by Vercingetorix vaulted Celtic Gaul over France's Latin heritage. Pétain, in a happier time a hero of the First World War, would be the modern Vercingetorix, that chief of the Averni tribe (c. 82 – 46 BC) credited with uniting the Gauls only to fall eventually to the Romans. In response, the conflicted philosopher of *Action Française*, Charles Maurras, wrote, "The civilization of Rome brought us too many things for it to be possible for us to repudiate it." Tragic in his ambivalence, and blind to his own racial mysticism, he would be sentenced in 1944 to life imprisonment as a collaborator, with his seat in the *Académie française* declared vacant. He died in 1952 at the age of eighty-two, still insensible to reason and convinced that his degradation was "Dreyfus's revenge."

The poet and diplomat, Paul Claudel, would feel the lash of the extremists. When his thirteenth grandchild was named Marie-Victoire, as she had been born on the day of the Allied landings in North Africa, the romantic monarchists of *Action Française* objected: "What! You choose the name of Victory for a girl born on the day on which we lose our African territories." Such were the priorities of this integralist counterrevolutionary movement of Maurice Pujo and Charles Maurras, eager to blame calamity on Jews and Freemasons. Pope Pius XI condemned *Action Française* in 1926, but Pope Pius XII lifted the penalties in 1939. Marcel Déat, a Vichy collaborationist and conflicted "rightwing neo-socialist," turned on Maurras and the *Action Française* as being insufficiently anti-democratic. Maurras had actually criticized the Vichy government's Statute on Jews in 1940, which denied French Jews full citizenship, as too moderate; but this was not strong enough for Déat, who mocked Maurras as a monarchist, responsible for scuttling the French fleet at Toulon.

As an invention constantly reinvented by French public intellectuals, *Action Française* has a history fraught with layers of inconsistent theories shingled one upon another. While Maurras supported Philippe Pétain's racism, he objected at least in theory to Vichy's German alliance. Some *Action Française* members – including Henri d'Astier de la Vigerie, Honoré d'Estienne d'Orves, and Pierre Guillain de Bénouville – joined the Resistance at home or fled and joined the Free French Forces. After the Liberation, Maurras and Déat were convicted for collaboration with the enemy. Maurras's life sentence was lifted when he became gravely ill, and he died in Tours in 1952, returning to his early Catholic faith after his agnostic years. Sentenced to death in absentia, Déat had fled to Germany after the Normandy invasion, where he was received by Hitler, and eventually died in the shelter of a monastery outside Turin under an assumed name in 1955.

Archbishop Saliège of Toulouse sent a message of condolence to the Chief Rabbi of Toulouse with reference to the deportations of Jews. Then on Sunday, September 6, he preached in his cathedral at the 8 o'clock Mass, regretting that the right of sanctuary had been abolished. Had the right still existed, he would have sheltered hunted Jews in his cathedral. Police arrived in time to prevent him from preaching at the 10 o'clock Mass. A spokesman on Radio Paris referred to the incident: "Tonight, my dear friends, I am going to deal with a painful subject. I am going to indict a Prelate and Prince of the Church, whom I consider to have exceeded his rights by recently adopting an attitude which is contrary to the directives of the Government, because it might hamper the progress of the Revolution. I am going to speak about Jules Saliège, Archbishop of Toulouse . . . It is not a question of persecuting the Jews, but of getting rid of them. It is a question of disinfecting France of a race which considers itself superior and whose natural rapacity, lack of scruples, excessive ambitions and desire to seize all the riches of the world, have at all times subdued the peoples who, like our own, committed the supreme error of welcoming it, sheltering it, defending it up to complete assimilation."

In response to the Brazilian declaration of war, Argentina's opposition to the Axis became louder with the encouragement of the auxiliary bishop of Buenos Aires, Msgr. Miguel de Andrea. President Castillo sent him to the United States to get diplomatic advice from the Roosevelt administration. While two soi-disant Catholic dailies, *Pueblo* and *Crisol*, were pro-Axis (the latter's editor, Enrique Oses, was openly Nazi), the democratic journal *Orden Cristiano* received support from many Latin hierarchs. The Bishop of Ayacucho, Peru, praised its "highly moral work" and envisioned "a new day which will triumph over the clouds which hell has spread over the world." For such bishops, racialism was "the somber menace of the world today."

The British government expressed concern about a declining population. The Lambeth Conference of the Anglican Communion had given a positive nod to artificial contraception in 1930. While there were some six million children in English and Welsh schools in 1942, it was predicted that the number would fall to four million by 1950 and slightly more than three million by 1960. This was quite off, as by 2010 there were slightly under eleven million children in England and Wales, but these make up only one-fifth of an aging population. The numbers are inflated by a rising tide of immigrants, which was not anticipated at all in

1942. Nonetheless, a book, *Parents Revolt*, called contraception "a great democratic freedom" and declaimed, "Women cannot enjoy the things of the mind, or play any part in democratic self-government, if the best twenty years of their lives are given up to the drudgery of the home." Meanwhile, 223,525 replies to a survey of the Commissariat Française de la Famille agreed that a parallel decline in the French birth rate was due to diminishing religious belief.

After the occupation of Yugoslavia in July of the previous year, the Germans and Italians had partitioned the Catholic land of Slovenia. In the German zone, only nine of 193 priests remained after a year, and these were elderly, leaving a quarter of a million Catholics without the Sacraments. The Italian archbishop of Gorizia, adjacent to the occupied diocese of Ljubljana, sent an unprecedented protest against the Axis troops to the Italian government and to the Holy See. The archbishop had previously been formally supportive of the Italian government, but in his protest he asked that the Fascist Militia in Slovenia be replaced by a civil administration.

In mid-September, Vatican Radio broadcast in German a pastoral letter of the German bishops dated "from the tomb of St. Boniface, August 19th, 1942." The Church had to "pass through a severe Calvary. . . . It has the courage of truth and faith in the fight for the liberty of conscience, for human dignity and for liberty in exercising the rights given to man by God and nature. . . . Not all Catholics are worthy members of the Holy Church . . . . Our enemies need not point this out to us again and again with malignant pleasure." On the day the bishops spoke out, the mostly Canadian forces in the British raid on Dieppe were almost entirely killed or captured by the Germans. The Vatican broadcast included a not insignificant aside of the bishops: "During these days, we have been occupied with serious questions and immediate anxieties, and we considered it our sacred duty to turn to the competent authorities. However, in this time of difficulties of war (*Kriegsschwer*), we do not think it appropriate to give further details in this episcopal letter."

While all this was unfolding, and the siege of Stalingrad continued with unspeakable suffering, a Requiem Mass was celebrated for Archbishop Stanisław Gall, administrator of the Archdiocese of Warsaw. At the height of the terror during the German occupation, he had been instructed by the government to issue a pastoral letter calling on all Poles to obey the German authorities, to which the archbishop replied, "I am a disciple of Jesus Christ, but I am not a Judas."

6. Just Because You're Paranoid

A September article in *De Misthoorn*, a Dutch Nazi Journal, scorned plutocracy as an enemy of National Socialism. The Nazi Party, representing the socialism of the masses, declared itself more hostile to capitalism than to Marxism, because the latter was based on "sounder principles." Nonetheless, Bolshevism in the Soviet Union was collapsing under the hammer blows of the German forces and would not prevail in post-war Europe, even if Communism should ever succeed in making America its second stronghold.

In this pastiche of reality, the ancillary threats to Nazism were Judaism and Freemasonry. In Europe, "Jewry" was being exterminated, and wherever the cleansing process may have been retarded by the war, the argument went, it would by and by be resumed and finished with redoubled vigor and thoroughness. Freemasonry would be a more intractable problem, because it was more scattered and clandestine. As the Freemasons were not generally considered inferior by race, they might be given another chance. In a victorious Nazi world, it would be essential to exclude from leading positions all those who had at any time belonged to Masonic societies, unless one had sound guarantees that the Masonic past of those persons would indeed remain a thing of the past.

"Greater than any other danger" to the progress of Nazism was the menace that *De Misthoorn* accorded an exclamation mark: "Jesuitism!" It behooved the "Fog Horn" to warn the public, with a paranoia redolent of late Tudor England and modern China, that Jesuitism had gained influence, unnoticed by the guileless citizen, and was the strongest weapon of the "Roman

Church" in propagating cultural products of a foreign race. The "International Holy Church" represented an age-long and fanatical Oriental and southern penetration, but its monuments in Germanic lands were eroding. *De Misthoorn* claimed proof that the Jesuits were fighting at the side of Jewry, Freemasonry, Bolshevism, and capitalism to break the German sword. Due to their "craftiness," the word "Jesuit" became "a synonym for Jew" but they were also tethered to Bolshevism, so the Jesuit was the "false comrade." As adjectives for craft and subtlety, "Jew" and "Jesuit" are synonymous. "And the strength of Jesuitism lies in its mysteries, its being invisibly present everywhere, its crafty and smooth penetration into the lives of communities, its undermining of all non-Catholic cultural and political activity."

Inflaming this rampant phobia, the 81-year-old auxiliary bishop of Paris, Bishop Emanuele-Anatole-Raphaël Chaptal de Chanteloup, publicly wore a Star of David in protest against the treatment of Jews. He had begun to see firsthand what he had earlier found incredible, when Jews began to be sent to Auschwitz from Paris in the Vel d'Hiv deportations of July. On September 12 – ten days after German troops entered Stalingrad – exiled Poles and Belgians sent a plea to the Pope to condemn Nazi war crimes. Although there was no action, the previous year Pope Pius XII had strongly condemned the racial legislation of the new pro-Nazi republic of Slovakia. On September 30, the German SS began mass executions of 3,500 Jews in Lodz, Poland, lasting six weeks.

Six years before, Father Hans Ansgar Reinhold, a liturgical scholar and student of Romano Guardini at Freiburg, escaped the Gestapo. He traveled from country to country to expose the Nazis, hindered somewhat by his reputation as romantic and even radical in liturgical matters, his chief cause being the celebration of the Holy Eucharist facing the people. In an article in the journal "Orate Fratres" in 1940, he described the "Dream Mass" that he had been promoting in the 1930s: "The altar was a stone table with low candlesticks. The priest stood behind it facing his flock, as is done in Rome and many other churches in the old country, especially Belgium and Germany." He hoped that such would be the common scene in the 1960s. He found Bishop de Chanteloup at first skeptical of his descriptions of the gestating Holocaust in Germany and was disappointed that Eugenio Cardinal Pacelli gave him little attention. Theodore Cardinal Innitzer thought him "an excitable émigré" In the United States, he was welcomed by Dorothy Day, but James Francis McIntyre (the vicar general of New York under Patrick Cardinal Hayes, and the future Cardinal Archbishop of Los Angeles) forbade him to speak publicly, and in Boston he found William Cardinal O'Connell frankly sympathetic toward Mussolini and Hitler. He would next be scandalized and then saddened when his friend Martin Heidegger and his wife, whom Heidegger had married in 1917, became Nazi propagandists. One of Father Reinhold's academic colleagues, Dietrich von Hildebrand, was condemned to death by the Nazis in absentia. Among other fellow Catholic scholars, Joseph Schmidlin was killed in a concentration camp, and Max Metzger and Alfred Delp were executed. Karl Rahner did not choose the martyr's path, slipping into unobtrusive retreat and making no public objections to the distress around him. In later years when the clouds had cleared, he confessed: "We should have done more to protect the skins of other people." As Bishop de Chanteloup was taking a stand in his old age, the Vichy broadcasts on "Radio Revolution" mocked Cardinal Gerlier of Lyons as "an ex-lawyer who late in life became an archbishop thanks more to the omnipotent grace of the House of Rothschild than to the laws of Holy Mother Church." Marshal Pétain's spokesman urged the cardinal to move to the mists of London and join "the anti-France triumvirate – Churchill, Cripps, and de Gaulle." Other prelates were better regarded: The controlled Radio Paris claimed that a message of loyalty to Pétain from the bishops of Provence had been endorsed by the Holy Father in a recent public utterance, a statement denied by the Nuncio. The government found rich propaganda in the message signed by the bishops: "The adherence of the Catholic clergy to the new regime, unmistakably approved by the Holy

Father in a recent public utterance, is all the more desirable since certain religious circles occasionally show a regrettable indulgence towards the former regime and those who dream of restoring it. Moreover, the message sent to the Marshal by the Archbishop of Aix and the Bishops of the Midi is no exception. Only last week, from the hill of Notre Dame de Lorette, at the other end of France, Msgr. Dutoit, Bishop of Arras, spoke words of special significance just now. Enjoining complete obedience to the civil authorities, 'we must,' he said, 'be obedient in our daily life and work, as was Christ. We shall also, as citizens, obey the revered leader whom Providence has put at the head of our country in this difficult time.' Thus the fundamental virtue of obedience has been twice enjoined within a few days upon French Catholics by the voice of those in special authority. May these exhortations recall some souls that have gone astray and preserve them in the future from doubt and error." In a pastoral letter the previous year, Bishop Henri Dutoit had said, "Collaboration is no slavery." When the Vatican defended Bishop Dutoit in 1944, the newly-dubbed Sir D'Arcy Osborne, British emissary to the Holy See, thought the Pope must have been greatly misinformed. At the liberation in 1945, Bishop Dutoit was the first collaborationist hierarch put in an internment camp. The Pope removed him from his diocese in November, 1945.

Because Italians traveling with German troops in Poland expressed horror at the public beatings and shootings that they frequently saw on railroad platforms, German authorities ordered trains with Italian passengers to stop at stations only briefly. The "Sonderdienst" (Special Troops) were becoming increasingly offensive in their attempts to exterminate Poles. Germans comprised their captains, but their numbers mostly were made up of Ruthenians, Ukrainians, Estonians and Latvians. Their strategy was to start pogroms by roaming through the streets trying to instigate arguments among the people, who would then be led off and shot without trial. In Warsaw, groups of citizens were piled into trucks with no explanation given, and not seen again. Special targets were priests, Jews and Polish reserve officers, the latter often shot in groups.

As the screed in *De Misthoorn* was ranting, the Nazi weekly *Volk en Vaderland* reported that German authorities in Holland had been forced to take several Catholic priests and aldermen as hostages. At Vlaardingen and Gorkum, the parish priests were taken as hostages. In the small region of Biereck, with only a population of 16,500, there were six churches and five monasteries, which the Nazis suspected as being centers of subversive instruction.

In Westminster, Cardinal Hinsley condemned anti-Semitism in a statement he signed along with the Archbishop of Canterbury, the Moderators of the Church of Scotland, the Free Church Federal Council, and the Chief Rabbi of the United Hebrew Congregations of the British Empire. The Republic of Ireland, invoking independence and neutrality, did not join this public expression. Fifty-three years later, Taoiseach John Bruton would apologize for such silence. In 2003, Justice Minister Michael McDowell publicly regretted the "culture of muted anti-Semitism" that denied entrance to Jewish refugees. In the interest of not exacerbating the Axis powers, Eire censorship forbade publication in the Free State of news that a kinsman of Blessed (canonized a saint in 1975) Oliver Plunkett in the British Army (5th Brigade of the 1st South African Irish Regiment), Lance Corporal Oliver Grice Holroyd-Smith, had been captured in Italy. Cardinal Tisserant was arguing the officer's case through Vatican diplomatic channels on the grounds that he was a citizen of a neutral state. Cardinal Tisserant was anything but neutral himself: although he had been born in 1884, he still wanted to enlist in the French army at the outbreak of the war, but obeyed the Pope who retained him as head of the Vatican library.

Anticipating the maxim of our contemporary community organizers that you should never waste a crisis, an English Evangelical, A. J. Ferris, sold the 100,000th copy of his pamphlet claiming that Churchill's "V" sign for victory actually represented the handwriting on the wall in the book of Daniel, Chapter V.

"Mene, Mene, Tekel, Upharsin," – You have been weighed in the balance and found wanting. He saw in this the finger of God demanding, "How will the millions of Roman Catholics in the British Commonwealth and the United States come out of Babylon and become Protestant scriptural Christians?" His answer was that it will come about when Russian troops invade the Vatican and publish its archives. "This exposure, coupled with the glorious Biblical awakening, will put an end to the Church of Rome in the Commonwealth of Israel." The pamphlet was not translated into Dutch, French, Italian, and there was no desire to translate it into Polish.

7. No Longer on the Defensive

In the second week of October 1942, Stalingrad was still stand-ing, if cruelly battered after eighty days of siege and starvation. The Russian strategy of ferrying troops into Stalingrad from across the Volga had worked. In what seemed by contrast an entirely other world, Ottawa announced that U-boats had torpe-doed eleven vessels in the St. Lawrence Seaway. The Polish newspaper *Nowy Swiat* noted that the Germans had forbidden priests to wear crucifixes, since such was "not in harmony with the spirit of the age." All candlesticks and liturgical vessels in Polish churches were to be confiscated. The previous month, the head of the Czech Orthodox Church, Bishop Matthias Gorazd, was tortured and executed on charges of complicity in the May 27 attack on SS-Obergruppenführer Reinhard Heydrich, who died from his wounds on June 4. That Church was formally dis-solved, its revenues confiscated by the Reich in the first instance of the Nazis actually abolishing a Church. The Belgian Nazi paper, "Vol en Staat," intractable in its anti-clericalism, turned the attention of its October 1 issue to the convents. "We do not worry much about the attitude of these nuns, who have always shown an anti-Flemish attitude. When we come to power, their activities will belong to the past. The nuns must conform to the regulations of national and National-Socialist education, or they will be granted permission to go and plant potatoes. The French nuns will, of course, be returned to their beloved fatherland. The 'Dames de l'Instruction Chrétienne' are simply pro-British."

Catholic newspapers in England mentioned in passing the death of Rev. Leo Paul Ward, son of Wilfrid Ward and brother of Maisie. She and her Australian husband Frank would become prominent apologists and publishers in the post-war years. The 46-year-old priest had died during his return from Japan, where he had been a missionary. He had been educated at the Oratory School from 1908 to to 1912, and then in Oxford at Christ Church. Frail health prevented him from entering the religious life, but he was ordained for the Archdiocese of Westminster after studying in the home of his mother. An active missionary life in Japan belied his poor health. He supported himself in Japan by teaching English and became a well-known figure among the Catholics of Japan.

By this time, rationing and food shortages had become severe in Britain. In the ecclesiastical world, church suppliers strongly advised their clergy customers to replenish their stocks of altar wine immediately, thereby "helping transport and avoiding any delay in the execution of their orders at a later date." Because of the paper shortage, altar missals were in limited supply, and special application had to be made by postcard for no more than one copy per individual. Daily papers ran advertisements from the Ministry of Food, in which a caricature named Potato Pete gave recipes for replacing bread and saving shipping space for military cargo. By giving the body warmth, potatoes could also save coal for the war effort.

The Vatican Radio broadcast in German an attack on the German press, comparing it to "scorpions lurking in the darkness." The Nazi newspapers would make man "a mere brute and a tool of this contradictory propaganda which seeks good through evil, order through disorder, and human dignity trough its negation."

General Jan Smuts arrived in London from South Africa and echoed the optimistic tone of Winston Churchill's recent address in Edinburgh, as well as one of Franklin Roosevelt's "fireside chats" in which he described increasing odds against the Axis. Even the *Frankfurter Zeitung* admitted that "hopes are now centered on how the United States will lose the war, and not on how Germany will win it." General Smuts cited the importance of the combat in the African theater. Arthur Cardinal Hinsley published a long essay on the future of Africa in relation to the Atlantic Charter. He likened Africa to "a grand piano which has suffered from neglect or abuse. The white and black keys represent the European and Native Africans. Will they ever be made to produce harmony, and if so, how? A Nazi victory would be disastrous for the indigenous tribes, whom they call 'semi-apes.'"

Pope Pius XI had defended the equal capacity of the African, given equal opportunity. There were only about 430 Catholic priests in Africa; they faced a daunting array of 700 languages and populations diverse as Hottentots and Bushmen, Bantu, Nilotics, and the Madagascar people, who were in fact "not of Negro type but Malayan." In a period of transition, "outside control in Africa is a guardianship which will invite the progressive co-operation of the native population." Cardinal Hinsley quoted a letter of Roosevelt to the Catholic hierarchy of the United States: "In victory we shall seek the establishment of an international order in which the spirit of Christ shall rule the hearts of men and of nations." This would be achieved only through missionaries, who "had the largest share in promoting the moral and physical welfare of the native populations."

While the bishops of Provence, with the exception of the bishop of Marseilles, paraded no virtue in opposing the bitter tenure of the Vichy government, the bishop of Rodez in unoccupied France, Msgr. Charles Challiol, forbade his priests to participate in Pierre Laval's *"Légion des Combattants"*; and Pierre-Marie Theas, bishop of Montauban, called for "national liberation from the Swastika." He reiterated his pastoral letter of August 30 ordered to be read in every church and chapel of his diocese: "I proclaim the indignant protest of the Christian conscience, and I declare that all men, Aryan and non-Aryan, are brothers, because they have been created by the same God; that all men, whatever their race or religion, have the right to the respect of individuals and the State. Now these anti-Semitic measures are a violation of human dignity and an invasion of the most sacred rights of the person and the family." Translations of the full text of the September 12 pastoral letter of Archbishop Jules-Gerard Saliège of Toulouse were published in Britain in October: "Why is it that the right of asylum in our churches no longer exists? Why have we been vanquished? Almighty God, have pity on us. Our Lady, pray for France. In our dioceses heartbreaking scenes have taken place in the camps of Noe and Recebedou. Jews are men and women. Foreigners are men and women . . . They are members of the human race. They are brothers as much as any others. No Christian must forget that. France, my beloved Fatherland, France which, in the conscience of all her children, carries on the tradition of respect for the human being, chivalrous and generous France, I am convinced you are not responsible for these horrors."

In unoccupied France, pastoral letters of the bishops were censored in the government press. In occupied France an opposite strategy was used: statements of the bishops were publicized as part of an offensive against the Church. Although Cardinal Gerlier was Primate of Gaul and the entire hierarchy of the Occupied Zone supported him, the Vichy government described them as "isolated" voices and made much of a letter of Provencal loyalty to the regime by the Archbishop of Aix, the bishops of Fréjus, Nice and Monaco, and the abbots of Lérins and Frigolet. No mention was made of the refusal of the bishop of Marseilles, the largest town in Provence, to sign it.

When words failed, Bishop Felix Roeder of Beauvais chose another course. German officials had ordered the Jews of Beauvais to register at the municipal headquarters. On the strength of his claim to have had a distant Jewish ancestor, the bishop formally processed through the streets to register his own name, wearing full pontifical vestments, and preceded by an acolyte carrying the Cross.

Flaunting his recidivist insensibility to reason, Joseph Goebbels ordered the Nazi Party Department for Public Enlightenment to publish ten million copies of a pamphlet for distribution in Europe and Latin America, condemning the Vatican's attempt to protect Jews. The pamphlet said that eighteen Popes since the twelfth century had promoted policies similar to that of the Nazi Party, but only Pope Pius XII had intervened on behalf of the Jews, and much of the Catholic world would turn against him. The London *Jewish Chronicle* wrote: "The extreme Nazi organs in Germany have been expressing great dissatisfaction at concessions made to the Vatican during the past two months which have enabled about 300 Jews to leave Nazi-occupied countries, including the ghettoes of Poland, and go to Spain and Portugal. The Vatican appears to have obtained Spanish and Portuguese visas for these Jews." Presumably in response, the Boston *Pilot* quoted Pope Gregory the Great: "We forbid you to molest the Jews or to lay upon them restrictions not imposed by the established laws; we further permit them to live as Romans and to dispose of their property as they will; we only prohibit them from owning Christian slaves." The *Pilot* also listed among protectors of the Jews Popes Sixtus IV, Clement VII, Eugenius III (encouraged by St. Bernard), Gregory IX, and Pius XI, who "defied Mussolini – and that at a time when the Italian dictator was 'monarch of all he surveyed' – when he said that 'spiritually we are all Semites.' Pope Pius XII crystallizes this defiance by the employment of Jewish scholars in the Vatican library. The brave defense of these harassed people by the French Hierarchy sustains a consistent, very noble tradition."

In Italy there was a new diatribe in the *Regime Fascista* in response to anti-Fascist cells forming in parish churches under the aegis of the Vatican. "No one will ever persuade us that *L'Osservatore Romano* and its Editor, an old acquaintance of the most pig-headed political world leaders, and his four sectarian adherents, with their anti-Fascist rancor, represent the Church. Less than ever do they represent it today, since this daily paper, with its partisan and ambiguous attitude, sows so much confusion in the consciences of patriotic Catholics, and has become the favorite reading matter of all the Masonic dark corners of the anti-Axis front. It is deplorable and highly ingenuous that there should be some Italian believers who, in their desire to discredit the sacrosanct war of the Axis, willingly have recourse to the inventions of the famous Anglo-Saxon propaganda, which has succeeded in creating a 'lamb-like' Bolshevism, a 'philanthropic' Judaism, and a 'civilizing' democracy." Later in October, it was learned that the writer of these words was a priest, Ettore Civati. The Bishop of Como, invoking Article 1386 of the Code of Canon Law, which forbids priests to write to newspapers without permission from their superiors, suspended Father Civati. Soon after, the Italian Ambassador to the Holy See formally protested a sharp criticism of "certain Fascist tendencies" preached by Cardinal Massimo Massimi, President of the Pontifical Commission for the Interpretation of Canon Law.

8. Two Crosses Raised against Each Other

In Parliament, Edward Tunour, the 6th Earl Winterton, remarked that Muslims did not like the Allies calling the war a "Christian Crusade," as both terms were odious to them. Lord Halifax and Sir Samuel Hoare both had described the war as a Christian struggle against evil. This was a sensitive matter since, while there was no significant Islamic population in Great Britain or the United States, they made up a third of the population in the Soviet Union, and many were elite troops in the Red Army. One MP, Reginald Sorenson, a Unitarian clergyman, endorsed Lord Winterton on the grounds that, first, considering the Soviets to be atheists, non-Christians among the Allies outnumbered Christians 3 to 1, and second, Britain was hardly Christian since only about twenty per cent of the population worshipped regularly. Sorenson had supported the Republicans in the Spanish Civil War and frequently demonstrated for Indian independence.

Italian Fascists observed the 20th anniversary of their movement, with Milan as its stronghold and Genoa a center of some resistance. A royal decree at the behest of the Germans had ordered that church bells be requisitioned and melted down for armaments, and the *Regime Fascista* denounced a parish priest in Bergamo who preached against turning the bells into "instruments of death" and added, "It is all the more sad because this measure is not so much desired by our government, but is imposed upon them by the Government of Luther's country. Today there are two crosses raised against each other: the Cross of Christ the King, and the crooked cross." The cardinal-archbishop of Milan ordered that it would be better to have silence than to simulate the sound of the missing bells with records and loudspeakers. In Rome, the president of the Pontifical Commission for the Interpretation of Canon Law mounted the pulpit of the Church of Sant'Andrea and preached with such animation against Fascist policies that the Italian ambassador to the Holy See sent a formal protest to the Pope.

Arthur Cardinal Hinsley dedicated All Saint's Day as a time of special prayer for the people of Czechoslovakia, where many priests continued to be killed in "reprisals" for the June 4 death of Reinhard Heydrich in Prague, where as *Stellvertretender Reichsprotektor* (Deputy Reich-Protector) of Bohemia and Moravia he had vowed to "Germanize the Czech vermin." The towns of Lidice and Ležáky were obliterated, and 13,000 Czechs were killed in the retaliatory massacres. A Catholic priest in Ždánice, named Father Kostiha according to the Nazi paper "Prager Abend," had sheltered several accomplices of a parachutist dropped by the British, and was taken into their confidence as they plotted sabotage. Father Kostiha and his curate, Father Vones, were executed on July 1. The papers included that item in a list of many other executed priests: "The spirit animating Kostiha does not seem rare among the Roman Catholic clergy in Moravia." A principal target of the Nazis was the Premonstratensian monastery of Neureisch. Another priest, Adolf Tesar, was sentenced to death for providing Jews with forged baptismal certificates. The killing of Heydrich had secured no particular military advantage. Evidently, the British intelligence had permitted Czech commandos to proceed with the assassination because Heydrich was suspicious of Admiral Wilhelm Canaris, formerly a German spy in Spain and now a counter-spy and source of military intelligence to the Allies.

Of a Northern Italian line, his Catholic grandfather having become a Lutheran, Canaris had dissuaded Franco from allowing German troops to attack Gibraltar through Spain. According to testimony later from the son of his assistant, Colonel Wessel von Freytag-Loringhoven, Canaris foiled Hitler's attempt to kidnap or assassinate both Pope Pius XII and King Victor

Emmanuel after the 1943 arrest of Mussolini at the king's orders. At a meeting in Venice, on July 29-30, 1943, as the Japanese were taking the strategically important site of Kokoda which gave access to Port Moresby, and the ground forces at El Alamein were at a stalemate, Canaris divulged the plot to the Italian general Cesare Ame. Eventually, on April 9, 1945, in the waning hours of the Reich, Hitler had Canaris hanged on the gallows at Flossenburg, naked, along with the theologian Dietrich Bonhoeffer and other resistance leaders. Historian Owen Chadwick maintained that the plot to kidnap and perhaps kill the Pope was a fabrication of British war propaganda, but a foreign correspondent for *The Washington Post*, Dan Kurzman, wrote a book "A Special Mission" three years before his death in 2010, based on interviews with SS General Karl Wolff, a former aide to Himmler, giving details of what he claimed was indeed an actual plot, although Wolff claimed that he was the principal agent in preventing it.

In the Pacific Islands, the Japanese were executing missionary priests and nuns. By the end of October, the European press had received news of the deaths of the vicar apostolic of New Guinea, Bishop Arnoldus Aerts, age 70, and a group of his missionaries who were massacred at Langpoer. Other missionaries, including an American, the Reverend Arthur Duhamel, were bayoneted on Guadalcanal.

Following the apparently effective abolition of the Czech Orthodox Church, the Nazis turned their attention to Poland and confiscated the property of the Archdioceses of Poznan and Gniezno. The plan was to replace the Church in those districts with "religious associations" subject to police control, leasing churches from the German State. Nearly 655,000 Polish civilian workers seized and taken to Germany were allowed religious services only on the first Sunday of each month, but both the Polish language and the solemnization of marriage were forbidden.

At the end of October, Cardinals Pierre-Marie Gerlier of Lyons and Emmanuel Suhard of Paris appeared with Philippe

Pétain at a ceremonial military review in Vichy along with the papal nuncio, who then immediately left for Rome. Cardinal Gerlier was particularly vexatious to the Vichy government, since he was, by virtue of being archbishop of Lyons, the primate of France. Collaborationists said a more accurate title for the primate of the Gauls would be "Primate of the Gaullistes." Having left Pétain, Cardinal Gerlier made a public visit to the editorial offices of the anti-Fascist paper *La Croix*, which received most of its news directly from the Vatican, and praised it in words understood as an attack on the Vichy press. Father Leon Merklen, editor of *La Croix*, warned against "those fanatics who set up new destructive ideas in the place of spiritual renaissance."

L'Osservatore Romano praised *La Croix* and reproached the collaborationist *L'Effort*. The Vatican newspaper also printed a speech of Jozef-Ernest Cardinal van Roey to the Belgian Young Christian Workers decrying the destruction of the Church in Luxembourg and the expulsion of nuns from the Duchy, but his principal case was against the use by the Nazis of the term "political Catholicism" to describe the Church's defense of her rights against the state. *L'Osservatore* belatedly reported that Father Maximillian Kolbe, O.F.M., publisher of *Maly Dziennik* and other journals, had died in Auschwitz. German authorities sent his habit to the monastery at Niepokalanów with a note that he had died in 1941 on August 14, without giving a cause, and that his remains had been cremated.

In November, the Swiss *National Zeitung* published the text of a telegram sent jointly by the Catholic hierarchy and Protestant leaders of Holland to their *Reichskommissar*, saying they were "deeply shocked by the measures against the Jews in the Netherlands," which cause a suffering that "goes against the deepest moral consciousness of the Dutch people." The Nazi *Deutsche Zeitung in den Niederlanden* reported that, in consequence of a pastoral letter of the bishops reiterating the substance of the telegram, German authorities "were bound to consider Roman Catholic Jews as their worst enemies, and had immediately sent them to the East." The cemeteries of Heerlen and Heerlerheide were closed on All Souls' Day to prevent prayers for the war dead.

At this time, an English translation of an historical novel was published, written by Franz Werfel, who had been born in Prague when it was part of the Austro-Hungarian Empire and had married the widow of Gustav Mahler after she divorced Walter Gropius. A Jew, Werfel had fled the *Anschluss* and sought refuge at the shrine in Lourdes. Solaced by various religious orders there, he completed his work called *The Song of Bernadette*. In the 1930s, Werfel had written essays one of whose themes was the perplexity of Jews seeking baptism and the ambiguity of reasons for doing so. He compiled them in 1944 under the title, "Zwischen oben und unten" – "Between Heaven and Earth." There is no evidence that he ever was baptized, but several Armenian Benedictine monks of the Meckhitarist monastery in Vienna, including the abbot Mesrop Habozian, insisted that he had received the sacrament. His association with the Armenian people began with the 1933 publication of his book "Forty Days at Musa Dagh" which made many in the West for the first time aware of the slaughter of 5,000 Armenians by Muslim Turks in 1915.

Lord William Birdwood, commander of the Australian and New Zealand Army Corps (ANZAC), commented on the fighting in Tunisia and Britain's approaching engagement of its Eighth Army at the naval base of Bizerta. He invoked ancient parallels with Crécy and Poitiers and, in the case of the ongoing siege of Stalingrad, he recalled the effect of weather on the Dutch fleet in 1795, when it was frozen and seized by the French in the only instance of cavalry capturing an entire Navy. But he did not have to reach far back for the First World War, in which he had been a general (and which was only half as far removed from the North African campaign as we now are from the Vietnam War). Having commanded the Australian and New Zealand armies at Gallipoli, his memory was fraught with the unspeakable losses of the "Great War," and such experience was what had made another war such a forbidden contemplation in the 1930s. The field marshal marveled that Eugene Rommel had started in October with no more than 100,000 troops, which was a size smaller than any similar campaign in the last 200 years. Compared with losses in the First World War, the 75,000 of Rommel's men killed, wounded, or captured seemed surprisingly small. As a soldier, the Baron Birdwood had gone to Australia to dedicate the Arch of Victory in Ballarat, and, as a scholar, he was Master of Peterhouse in Cambridge. Born in Khadki, India, he died in Kensington Palace; his field marshal's baton is in the Australian Military Museum, a memento of a most storied symbol of the British Empire.

The University of Oxford announced that it would confer the degree Doctor of Civil Law, *honoris causa*, on Cardinal Hinsley on December 12. Although there was an RAF airbase at nearby Abingdon, German planes always avoided the university on their bombing runs to Coventry and other industrial areas. It was said that Hitler expected Oxford to make him a Doctor of Civil Law after he had won the war.

9. Spiritual U-boat Action

The Pope announced as his November intention for prayers: "The preservation of the true Faith in Europe." The Vatican wireless on August 6, in German, said: "God's ship is destined to reach port safely. She will not sink, for Christ is the helmsman and the gates of Hell, the onslaught of the wildest waves and of the spiritual U-boat action ('Geistige U-boot Arbeit') of godless neo-paganism will not harm her. . . . Neo-paganism does not only intend to destroy the most precious treasures and fruits of the one and undivided great and holy truth; it wants to extend its own sphere, to put something else in the place of true faith – an 'ersatz' religion. It is something which one cannot really call by a positive name. For while paganism cannot build up, still less can neo-paganism, which lacks even that nobility of mind and true humanity which was found in the old pagans."

As if to confirm the Pope's imputation of neo-paganism to the culture of National Socialism, a new play by the Nazi dramatist Otto Erler premiered in Dresden at the Staatliche Schauspielhaus. The play, "Not Gottes," was the second of a trilogy about "the ideological conflict between Christianity and the Germanic tradition." The first play, produced in 1938, was "Thors Gast" and the third, not yet complete, was to be called "Thor und der Krist." Erler died in 1943, with the trilogy unfinished. Long before the Nazis, in 1903, he wrote an anti-Semitic play as an enthusiast of the Nationalist movement. The Dresden premier had been preceded by a private performance in Berlin for members of the Waffen-SS, at the end of which an SS leader thanked the playwright for "his contribution to the spiritual education of our people."

In Leipzig, *Das Deutsche Tuberkulosenblatt* described the forced detention in State hospitals of infectious cases of pulmonary tuberculosis. Those who did not fit the correct political profile were sent to a special pavilion where no treatment was given. "Nothing is done to arrest the course of the disease and thus to prolong a life which is of no value to the community. There are only male nurses in this section, and they now carry revolvers as a precautionary measure, since in the past patients have frequently assaulted the nurses." This report was proudly written by Dr. Gerhart Kloos, whose distinguished studies in tuberculosis infection had gained an international reputation by 1938. He also supervised a "Kinderfachabteilung," or children's ward, in Stadtroda, Thuringia which was in fact a clinic for euthanizing handicapped children.

Celebrations had been planned in France for November 14 and 15, the sixth centenary of the election of Pope Clement VI, Pierre Roger, formerly bishop of Rouen. Radio Lyons had encouraged a large attendance and the Papal Nuncio was to attend. The festivities were more than a celebration of Frenchness. Though given to a style of lavish living which Plutarch may have exaggerated, Pope Clement was conspicuous in papal history for his benevolent custody of Jews. In 1348, when the Jews were accused of responsibility for the Black Death, hysteria spread and more than 18,000 were massacred in Bavaria, Brussels, Basel and Mainz. Clement VI issued Bulls for their protection, excommunicating anyone who attacked them, and granting them refuge in Avignon. Without explanation, the celebrations were cancelled on German orders.

On November 17, 1942, as the Japanese were sending reinforcements into New Guinea, the Catholic publisher Wilfred Meynell celebrated his 90th birthday in quiet Greatham, southwest of London. He would live another six years and, with the noise of RAF fighter planes a familiar sound daily, he could boast that he was born the year the Duke of Wellington died. Henry Edward Cardinal Manning fostered his literary career, and Meynell wrote lives of him and other contemporaries, including John Henry Cardinal Newman and Pope Leo XIII. His wife, Alice, who died exactly 20 years earlier, was the poet who had encouraged her fellow poet Francis Thompson in his struggle with opium addiction. Coincident with Meynell's birthday was the death of the Catholic convert F. W. Speaight, at the age of 74. The civil architect had designed the decorations for the funeral procession of King Edward VII in 1910 and five years earlier had renovated the Marble Arch.

In the Slipper Chapel of the Shrine of our Lady of Walsingham, a novena was planned before the Feast of the Immaculate Conception for the intention of Allied victory. Eastward, the Orthodox Churches were struggling with disorder. The Soviet Union had broadcast a message from the metropolitan of Moscow and de facto patriarch, Sergius, congratulating Joseph Stalin on the 25th anniversary of the October Revolution. Immediately after this, the Romanian Patriarch Nicodemus resigned. Just a few days later, the *Neue Zürcher Zeitung* in Zurich reported the resignation of the interim patriarch Nicholas Balan, metropolitan of Sibiu. The metropolitan of Bessarabia had resigned some months before that.

Romania was the only predominantly Orthodox country officially at war with the Soviet Union. While Sergius was recognized by the patriarchs of Antioch, Jerusalem, and Alexandria, German propaganda enjoyed publicity of him as a cooperative agent of the Bolsheviks in controlling the Romanian church. Shortly before his resignation, Nicodemus had offended the Soviets by reorganizing the Romanian province of Transnistria in Russian Ukraine. In an instance of thief catching thief, the Nazis quickly detected a work of cynicism and even a gesture of desperation in the Soviet pretense of reviving religion. Stalin was restoring church properties and granting concessions to Sergius, but at the price of his compliance.

By November, the Germans were on the defensive both in North Africa and around Stalingrad. A year before, Adolf Hitler had pledged that Moscow would be taken by the end of 1942. He and Nazi foreign affairs minister Joachim von Ribbentrop had predicted the fall of Stalingrad around the same time. They were not as prophetic as Charles de Gaulle, who had said that the battle for Africa would change the whole complexion of the war. As portents seemed more favorable, many ambiguous Frenchmen began to rally to the side of the Fighting French headquartered in London, calling to mind the parable of the laborers who came into the vineyard at the eleventh hour. If Admiral François Darlan had deployed the French fleet in favor of the Allies, General Archibald Wavell could have secured all of North Africa as early as 1940. But Darlan pleaded – falsely, in the estimation of the Allied forces – that he had been afforded no alternative.

Complicating loyalties was General Maxime Weygand, himself a conflicted man whose uncertain parentage was alternately said to have involved the Empress Carlota of Mexico and King Leopold II of the Belgians. His rarified Catholicism found early expression in opposition to the Dreyfussards and obsession with cabals of Protestants, Freemasons, and Jews. A credentialed foe of the Germans until 1940, he conveniently shifted sides and became a Pétainist and a chief Jew-baiter of the Vichy regime. Unrepentant, he died in 1965, nearly 100 years old, professing the Catholicism he had tried to redefine when it seemed unsympathetic to the throne-and-altar Catholicism of *Action Française*. That exotic cultural flower, urged by Maurice Pujo and Henri Vaugeois, actually envisioned the restoration of the monarchy with the Duc de Guise as king.

In 1942, the movement's apologist, Charles Maurras, himself vague in religious belief, collected statements of 39 French bishops supportive of Phillipe Pétain, but these were less than half of the entire French episcopate. Maurras did not mention the bishops of the Resistance: the Cardinal Archbishops of Lyons, Paris and of Lille, the Archbishop of Toulouse, the Ordinaries of Besancon, Bourges, Cambrai, Rheims, Rouen, Sens, Amiens, Angers, Angouleme, Arras, Autun, Bayonne, Beauvais, Blois, Chalons, Chartres, Coutances, Dijon, Evreux, Langres, Lucon, Le Mans, Meaux, Nantes, Nancy, Nevers, Orleans, Poitiers, Quimper, La Rochelle, Saint-Brieue, Seez, Soissons, Troyes,

Vannes, Verdun and Versailles. In bleak contrast, the Archbishop of Aix in mid-November sent a letter to Marshall Pétain, praising "the magnificent courage and firmness with which you are defending France's destiny" and on November 19, Msgr. Gounoud, Archbishop of Carthage and Primate of Africa, a fervent Pétainist of long standing, expressed, in a telegram to the Marshal, "his French loyalty, his respectful attachment, and his fervent prayers." Despite the condemnation of *Action Française* by Pope Pius XI, which had been rescinded by Pius XII as mentioned in Chapter 5, Maurras would influence extreme movements especially in Latin America. The rector of the French College in Rome, Father Henri Le Floch, who was greatly admired by his student Marcel Lefebvre, was removed from his office because of his sympathies for Maurras. Revanchism found a publicist in Jacques Marcy, who strongly resented how every Catholic family in Lyons sheltered a Jew. In Toulouse, Jewish children were hidden in Catholic schools. Another *Action Française* apologist, Marcel Déat, warned that the resistance of Catholics to the totalitarian spirit of "the New Europe" would result in a "terrible adventure."

Benito Mussolini was beginning to reap the whirlwind of having assisted the Germans in bombing England in 1940. While officials in the Italian government, and even some Catholic prelates, claimed that retaliatory raids by the Allies were unjustified, many of the Italian parochial clergy did not respond well to Fascist attempts to stir up hatred for the Allies. A parish priest of Monte di Nese near Bergamo, not unrepresentative of his fraternity, used his pulpit to excoriate the local military commander for pasting up posters reading, "Hate the British!"

On the more remote shores of the United States, the Administrative Board of the National Catholic Welfare Conference, over the signature of Edward Cardinal Mooney of Detroit, in a statement on "Victory and Peace," expressed concern about the neglect of children by mothers called up for work in war industries, and deplored the murderous assault upon Poland, "utterly devoid of any semblance of humanity" and the "premeditated and systematic extermination of the people of that nation. The same satanic technique is being applied to many other peoples. We feel a deep sense of revulsion against the cruel indignities heaped upon the Jews in conquered countries and upon defenseless people not of our faith." They declared solidarity with "our brother bishops in subjugated France." That was notwithstanding the division among the French bishops themselves about the nature and portent of such subjugation. The document spoke of "paternal solicitude for American Negroes," and also addressed the Bishops of Latin America: "We express the hope that the mistakes of the past which were offensive to the dignity of our southern brothers, their culture and their religion, will not continue. A strong bond uniting in true friendship all the countries of the Western Hemisphere will exercise a most potent influence on a shattered post-war world."

10. State Absolutism

St. Thomas More said that to be a Christian, we must not only believe the Resurrection, we must continually be surprised by it. That saint, surprised daily by the empty tomb, saw what happens when people are not even surprised by God, and wander in an abyss of cynicism. The reinvented government that sentenced More to death was, from various angles, a prototype of the all-inclusive state latterly called Fascist. For Fascism is authority run rampant for lack of an author, imposing a disorderly order instead of order itself. It is why the saint's dying words reminded the people that there is a distinction between service to the king and service to God.

Christopher Hollis reviewed for *The Tablet* a book by Josiah Wedgwood, lately 1st Baron Wedgwood, whose peerage Winston Churchill had helped secure. "Testament to Democracy," newly published in 1942 with a Foreword by Churchill, was about the perils of confusing God and King. Hollis – parliamentarian, old friend of G. K. Chesterton, Evelyn Waugh, and Msgr. Ronald Knox, and both son of an Anglican bishop and father of a Catholic bishop – stretched his gift for irony: "Lord Wedgwood is in the great tradition of English eccentrics. He is a writer and a speaker rather than a reader, and this preference gives him a fondness, in default of better, for talking about subjects about which he knows absolutely nothing."

One of these subjects was Fascism. Hollis says of Lord Wedgwood, "He is one of the last people left in Parliament who says what he thinks – or rather, to be quite frank, who says a great deal more than he thinks – and that, in this age of sealed lips, is at least a contrast to the many who say less." Hollis's point was that the author in his crosshairs fails to see that Fascism was latent in the democratic system, and what holds it back is the "aristocratic taste" for liberty among those with a sense of tradition and freedom from economic reliance on government assistance. "It is no coincidence that Fascism has made its appearance in the age of democracy," he went on. "As long ago as Plato the succession of the one to the other in invariable sequence was noted. Liberty is an aristocratic taste – the taste of men with independent incomes and a sense of tradition. If you want liberty, then you must tolerate the degree of inequality of income which is necessary to preserve such a class. If you destroy that class, then you hand over power to people who have no regard for liberty, and democracy rapidly collapses into what it is now the fashion to call Fascism. . . . Where there is no aristocratic element, you get just as much tyranny but no protest against it."

Hollis's complaint was not so much about Wedgwood's understanding of Fascism (both were strong opponents) and Wedgwood had in fact toured America as an opponent of appeasement. But Hollis objected to what he considered to be Wedgwood's unmeasured promotion of Zionism. For Hollis, "Lord Wedgwood's enthusiasm may easily cost us a Holy War throughout the whole of the Eastern world, death, murder, massacre and Armageddon. . . ." Wedgwood, the great-great grandson of the Unitarian potter who started the famous company bearing his name, was something of a romantic as a champion of the underdog, as in his publicity of Hungary's suppression of suspected Communism in the 1920s, his defense of radical immigrants like Emma Goldman, and the Indian independence movement. He resented the British partition of its territories into Palestine and Transjordan and especially objected to the restrictions on Jewish immigration there. He found it helpful to use the Nazi persecutions to argue for a more generous Jewish immigration policy.

In this he was opposed by another peer, the Anglo-Irish Walter Guinness, 1st Baron Moyne, British minister of state in the Middle East. In a speech in the House of Lords in June 1942, Lord Moyne had said: "The Government have already explained what has been done to arm the Jews for the legitimate purpose of self-defense, . . . but is it not clear that Lord Melchett and the responsible leaders of the Jews in this country generally seek to be saved from Lord Wedgwood in his attempt to make political capital out of the natural desire of the Jews to do their utmost to defend the cause of freedom against Nazi tyranny? . . . It must surely have a deplorable effect upon our Allies to be told by an ex-Cabinet Minister that the Palestine Administration do not like Jews, and that there are enough Anti-Semites in Great Britain to back up the Hitler policy and spirit. This suggestion is a complete reversal of the truth. If a comparison is to be made with the Nazis it is surely those who wish to force an imported régime upon the Arab population who are guilty of the spirit of aggression and domination. Lord Wedgwood's proposal that Arabs should be subjugated by force to a Jewish régime is inconsistent with the Atlantic Charter, and that ought to be told to America." In Cairo on November 6, 1944, Lord Moyne was assassinated by Eliyahu Hakim, a member of the radical Zionist group, Lehi.

In the first week of December, as English men of letters were discussing the etymology and portents of Fascism, a real Fascist with a megaphone, Mario Appelius, broadcast from Rome his aversion to understatement: "After the war, when people are heard speaking English in Italian towns, those around them will turn round sharply as if they heard the howling of a hyena or the hissing of a snake, and a light of hatred will go up in the eyes of the men and women of Italy." At least Signor Appelius was consistent. Back in October 1940 he had written that the United States would be committing suicide if it entered the war on the side of the British, and so its best hope would be early defeat of the British: "The speed of the Axis will probably save the American people from the great tragedy to which plutocracy has condemned it."

On December 8 in Westminster Cathedral, the Polish Bishop Karol Radonski celebrated Mass in the presence of Cardinal

Hinsley and representatives of the Polish Government in exile. The Germans had deported thirty-nine of Poland's forty-six bishops. Radonski was among those prelates in exile expressing frustration with Pius XII for not speaking out more strongly about the situation in their homeland, while those bishops remaining in Poland urged the Pope not to say anything that might only cause reprisals. Some of them, Polish officers, were resident in the London house of the abovementioned Lord Moyne near Buckingham Palace at 11 Grosvenor Place which he had made over to them for the duration. The Cardinal preached: "Here I unite my voice to the loud denunciation uttered by Catholic Bishops and peoples of France, Italy and other countries against the brutal persecution of the Jews. Poland has witnessed acts of such savage race hatred that it appears fiendishly planned to be turned into a vast cemetery of the Jewish population of Europe."

As the Fascist radio broadcast from Rome its summons to hate, the Vatican radio announced in German a summary of the joint pastoral letter of the archbishops and bishops of Austria (the "Greater Reich") on the "sexual revolution" of the Nazis, who encouraged immodesty and promiscuity in the name of liberation from Christian strictures. A similar pastoral letter had been written by the cardinal archbishop of Breslau in September. "There is a tendency gradually to do away with the essential segregation of sexes during youth meetings, by day and night and during lonely hiking tours and on similar occasions." They denounced the "naturalism" promoted by Nazi university professors, which taught that "natural functions," being "natural," should be freed from moral inhibitions. "The helplessness and inability of parents to control their children is also greatly to blame for this sad state of affairs."

The bishops also objected to the attempts of the government to defy natural law by making itself the sole arbiter of what constitutes marriage. "From this point of view it is merely another step to the monstrous idea of sexual relationship without recourse to marriage at all, and the scientific breeding of the superman. . . ." The bishops baldly and boldly declared: "A people that presumes to be the only and exclusive arbiter of morality, and goes to the length of sanctifying whatever means it adopts for its terrestrial purposes, must perish through its own blasphemy." The fantastic, indeed Gnostic, manipulation of natural law was ushered in by an equally unreal manipulation of language, and the road to eugenics was made smooth by euphemism. Only those who allowed themselves to be so manipulated could have failed to predict the inevitable result of it all: the stillbirth of a mythical superman.

A series of articles in *L'Osservatore Romano* treated the "menace to human liberty" posed by the secularist view of life. The distinction between the justice willed by God and positive regulations willed by human authority is evident in the various Latin and Germanic languages: "jus" and "lex," "recht" and "gesetz," "droit" and "loi," "diritto and "legge," "derecho" and "ley." The papacy has a unique position, divinely appointed, as arbiter in this economy of wills. The Reformation disrupted this, even altering the concept of the sacredness of treaty obligation, so that "from being something demanded from a nation on religious and moral grounds, it became something accepted because profitable or useful, claiming respect only in so far as it served that purpose."

A letter of June 14, but only translated and published in English in the beginning of December, was written by Msgr. Giuseppe Srebrenic, Bishop of Veglia, a Yugoslavian island in the northern Adriatic, to the Cardinal Secretary of State. In it he describes the numerous atrocities committed two months earlier by the Italian military and civil authorities among the Croat and Slovene populations annexed to Italy: homes laid waste, men of the villages arbitrarily shot, and many deported. "It is true that such happenings also take place among the German Nazis, but they profess pagan and materialist pagan principles, whereas the Italian people is wholly Catholic and the Italian Army is wholly Catholic, accompanied everywhere by a large number of Italian priests – military chaplains. Precisely in this fact lies the gravity of the situation, which is leading the Croat and Slovene peoples, in their despair, to the conclusion that Catholicism permits all the above-mentioned and similar cruelties, and has neither the will nor the power to resist them and to condemn them. Moved by such thoughts, and exposed also to the suggestions of agitators, the people are, alas, more and more losing trust in the Catholic Church and loyalty to the Holy Father; while on the other hand they are being thrown into the arms of Communism, in which they are beginning to see the only element which will defend them in the forests against the cruelty of the Italian elements."

In *The Tablet* in one of his weekly exegeses of the Advent readings for Mass, Monsignor Knox obliquely touched on how the Church herself can be arbitrary in prudential matters of positive law. Explaining the word "skandalizein" as "being thrown off your stride," or "disappointed," he says specifically for English readers, "The convert whose faith is tried by (say) finding himself in disagreement with Vatican policy, over European affairs, is a good instance of being 'scandalized' in this sense."

From Lourdes, which he called "Czestochowa in the Pyrenees," August Cardinal Hlond sent a message to the youth of Poland, among whom was an unknown named Karol Wojtyła:

> "The fate and future of Poland will shortly be in your hands. . . . Remember that it is the design of Divine Providence that you should be the builders of Poland's greatness. You will finish the building of the Commonwealth and you will lead our nation into the second thousand years of our history. Even now, you should give a lofty and Christian meaning to your life, a sense of mission, duty and responsibility. Feed yourselves with truth and not with phrases."

Both by default and generosity of spirit, the Catholics in the United States responded to the international chaos by assuming financial responsibility for nearly fourth-fifths of all the world's missions. An American chaplain was invited to preach in

Westminster Cathedral, and the *Daily Express* reported that "the sermon was given by one of the fastest speaking preachers ever to occupy the Cathedral pulpit." From the same pulpit, Cardinal Hinsley's Advent message was read more slowly:

> "We pray week by week and month by month at Benediction for the return of England to the unity of faith. In doing so we prolong the prayers which our own martyrs and which Catholics of nearly every country of Europe have offered decade after decade for this intention. . . . Surely this has been because England was regarded as a supremely important link in the spiritual harmony of Christendom. . . . We must resist to the last any system of State absolutism such as in other lands captures the bodies and souls of the children, thus usurping the rights and duties of the parents. We find it difficult to suppose that any party in this country would dream of such an invasion of the family."

But that difficulty of supposition, of course, was in 1942.

11. The Coming of Emmanuel

With the blackouts and bleak uncertainty about the fortunes of war, the days before Christmas were dark. The death of Father Wlodimir Ledóchowski, the "Black Pope," on December 13 somberly marked a period of impressive growth for the Society of Jesus, whose general he had been since 1915. Monuments to his service included new buildings for the Curia Generalis on Borgo Santo Spirito and the Gregorian University on the Piazza Pilotta, along with the Oriental Institute, the Russian College, and the Biblicum. His uncle, the Cardinal Archbishop of Gniezno, had been deposed one month after taking office in the Kulturkampf of April 1874, imprisoned for two years, and lived from then on in Roman exile. One of Father Ledóchowski's sisters would be beatified by Pope Paul VI, and another canonized by Pope John Paul II. The Father General was small in stature and frail in appearance: "In later years, his face had a certain ageless transparent look; and he walked with a noticeable limp."

Father Ledóchowski had supervised the Latin translation of Pope Pius XI's encyclical *Humani Generis Unitas*, which Eugene Cardinal Tisserant attested was on the Pope's desk the day he died on February 10, 1939. Tisserant could express himself in thirteen languages and was impatient with the customary diplomatic diction of Vatican documents which he regretted might be interpreted as more nuanced than prophetic. Under Father Ledóchowski's guidance, three Jesuits had drafted the document in Paris: the American John LaFarge, the German Gustav Gundlach, and the French Gustave Desbuquois. While the encyclical began with a general condemnation of modernist assumptions, it moved into a specific attack on racism, which is to secular progressivism what a doll is to an idol: the miniature of a big lie fit for small minds. Father LaFarge's hand was evident in the condemnation of American racial segregation, but the burden was anti-Semitism and Nazi eugenics. As it was never published, it has been called "The Hidden Encyclical," with the implication that Pope Pius XII found it too strong. Now we know that Pius XII, in his own inaugural encyclical *Summi Pontificatus*, took up the theme of race mythology but excised the glaringly anti-Jewish commentary that accompanied the broad condemnations of genocide in the text Father Ledóchowski had presented to Pius XI. The actual term "genocide," or a Latin equivalent, "parricidum generis," did not appear in any discourses at the time, as it was a neologism first used in 1944. In 1932, the poet August Graf von Platen used an equivalent in his disgust at the Russian "Volksmurder" in their repression of the Polish revolution of 1831. The Polish-American jurist, Raphael Lemkin, invented the word. Like Harry Truman, who had not been informed of the Yalta texts, Pius XII apparently had not previously seen the text of *Humani Generis Unitas*. Contrary to the claims of some later historians, Pius XII preserved the essential critique of anti-Semitism, while excising stereotypical descriptions of Jews that would have been exploited by the Nazis: "Blinded by a vision of material domination and gain," and "this unhappy people, destroyers of their own nation."

On December 21, Msgr. Jan Sramek, Prime Minister of the Czechoslovak Republic, celebrated the golden anniversary of his priestly ordination. Years before, he had combined political activity with his pastoral work as a parish priest and, in the Czech opposition to Hapsburg rule, he had opposed and later befriended Jan Masaryk. Largely through his witness, millions of Czech Catholics remained loyal to the Holy See when tempted to schism in the nationalist spirit of the young republic. In the 1920s, he had secured the Church's properties and canonical freedom and organized the Eucharistic Congress at Prague in 1935. In the 1939 Nazi invasion, at the age of 70, Monsignor Sramek refused to surrender and chose exile. He became prime minister when the

Allies recognized the Czechoslovak National Committee as the government in exile. After the war, he maintained leadership of the People's Party, but he would be deposed by the Communists in 1948, dying in 1956, ever the patriot and priest.

On December 12, as Rommel retreated to Tripoli from El Agheila in weather more tolerably warm, the former liner *S.S. President Coolidge*, appropriated by the War Shipping Administration for the U.S. Army, was sunk in the South Pacific with most of its crew saved; the Battle of Stalingrad was in full force; and Operation Winter Storm (*Unternehmen Wintergewitter*) was launched, in which the German Fourth Panzer Army attempted to relieve encircled Axis forces in bitter cold. On that same day, beset with severe food rationing, in a sandbagged Sheldonian Theatre in Oxford, an honorary degree was conferred on Arthur Cardinal Hinsley. The Deputy Public Orator began, *"Principes illustrissimos vel civitatis vel Ecclesiae ornare semper nos gavisi sumus, sed nullos, opinor, libentius ornavimus quam qui in altissimo dignitatis gradu collocati res magnas et excelsas non modo videre sed etiam aliis monstrare numquam desierunt"*:

> "The bestowal of honours on the most illustrious leaders both of Church and State has always been a joy to us. But on none, I think have we bestowed them more gladly than on those who, holding the highest place in dignity, have never ceased both to keep their own gaze fixed on the greatest and noblest realities and to make these known to others."

A few days before Christmas, having received more evidence of the systematic killing of European Jews, the entire British House of Commons rose to its feet in solemn protest. The Jewish historian Cecil Roth contrasted this genocide with the expulsion of the Jews from England in 1290 when King Edward I acted "with scrupulous fairness and almost humanity" with "public proclamations made in every county that no person should 'injure, harm, damage, or grieve the Jews' in the time which must lapse until their departure." The Board of Management of the Christian Council for Refugees from Germany and Central Europe expressed "its readiness to co-operate in every way within its power in any appropriate steps which may be taken to relieve any victims of this persecution who may succeed in making their escape."

The Axis powers, exploiting the shortage of food shipments from Marseilles to stir up anti-colonial sentiment, were surprised that the Muslims of North Africa were reluctant to cooperate with them. One reason was German discrimination against Arab prisoners of war, though the main reason was said to be a theological opposition to the incoherence of Nazi atheist mythology. In Morocco, King Muhammed V was especially opposed to Nazism, quietly assisting Jews. Most of the 14 million Muslims in French North Africa, however, identified with Vichy and only helped the Allied cause through the influence of Admiral Francois Darlan.

The situation was different in Syria, where Hitler was hailed as "Abu Ali" by the National Socialist Party. In Egypt, Hitler was "Muhammed Haidar" to the Young Egypt Party, one of whose members was Gamal Abdul Nasser. Sunni theological complaints with National Socialism did not overwhelm the Grand Mufti of Jerusalem in the British Mandate of Palestine, Haj Mohammed Effendi Amin el-Husseini, who eventually made his way to Berlin in 1941 where he consulted Hitler; visited Auschwitz to encourage the guards to work faster; secured the deportation of 5,000 Jewish children to death camps, having blocked Adolf Eichmann's proposed exchange of them for British-held German POWs; and obtained a promise from Hitler to liquidate the Jews of Palestine after a Nazi victory. In September 1943 he would block a plan to rescue 500 Jewish children in the Croatian town of Arbe by sending them to Palestine through Turkey, where the Apostolic Delegate and future Pope, Msgr. Giuseppe Roncalli, was aiding Jews. The Grand Mufti encouraged Muslims to join the Waffen SS and organized Arab students and North African émigrés into an Arab Legion in the German Army, the "Arabisches Freiheikorps," which fought on the Russian front and hunted down Allied parachutists in the Balkans. His commitments were summed up in an address given over Radio Berlin in 1944: "Arabs, rise as one man and fight for your sacred rights. Kill the Jews wherever you find them. This pleases Allah, history and religion. Allah is with you." Far from Syria, the Albanians, whose king was in exile in England, were told both by Mr. Eden for Britain and Mr. Cordell Hull for the United States that their governments wanted "to see Albania freed from the Italian yoke and restored to independence."

General Franco replied to Hitler's greeting on his birthday: "I send you my wishes for a triumph of German arms in the glorious enterprise of liberating Europe from the Bolshevik terror." Some analysts thought it significant that Franco limited his reference to the Russian campaign. Il Caudillo removed his brother-in-law, Serrano Súñer, from the Foreign Secretaryship when he expressed hopes for Axis success in Europe. The new foreign minister, Count Francisco Gomez-Jordana, helped to make Spain a haven for Eastern European Jews, especially Sephardic Jews from Hungary. Spanish Communists Isidora Ibárruri ("La Pasionaria") and Jesus Hernandez had taken refuge in Moscow, where they broadcast Marxist propaganda to Spain. While Spain remained officially neutral, Romania in 1940 ceded most of her western territory to Hungary and, under Marshal Ion Antonescu, gave German troops entry into Romania "for the purpose of instructing the Rumanian Army." Between the signing of the Vienna Diktat in 1940 and Christmas 1942, the total casualties in the Romanian army killed and wounded on the Eastern Front after "instruction" by the Germans was more than 350,000, a figure the Germans suppressed. King Carol had fled the country and Antonescu became the Nazi's puppet leader.

In Belgium, Louvain ceased to be a Catholic university, and students of the *Katholiek Vlaamsch Hoofstudentenverbond* were forbidden to begin the academic year with a Mass. In Hungary, Jusztinián Cardinal Serédi published extracts from the Joint Pastorals of the German bishops in his journal *Magyar Sion* and told members of the Stephan Academy in Budapest that "the most valuable right is human liberty, for which it has always paid to fight."

The Italian Fascist propagandist Farinacci blamed Allied bombings in Italy on a conspiracy of Myron Taylor, Winston Churchill, British Catholics, the Church of England, and the Vatican, which *L'Osservatore Romano* denied. Undeterred, Mussolini's spokesman said: "The Chair of St. Peter, which guides men to the kingdom of God and does not concern itself with temporal matters, is one thing; quite another thing is the Vatican State, which can engage in politics in the same way as Chiang Kai-shek, Haile Selassie, Churchill, and so on. And in politics there exists no infallibility."

So Christmas came, Emmanuel once made flesh abided "in agony until the end of the world." In the London papers, the confectioner De Bry de Paris, located at 64 New Oxford Street, ran an advertisement saying that their supply of chocolates had dwindled: "Therefore the many, who in the past delighted in the enjoyment of the De Bry quality, must of necessity be reduced to the fortunate few who can obtain them."

12. Ending a Year with No End in Sight

If the Third Reich did not style itself after the Babe of Bethlehem, Dr. Goebbels proposed some fugitive cheer in a radio broadcast on Christmas Day by changing the subject of the feast. He hailed the Japanese for being free of the remnants of Christianity that he regretted in his Fatherland. As he broadcast, the British were taking Libya and American bombers were attacking Rabaul in Papua New Guinea.

Goebbels told the German people: "It is our national misfortune that we could never muster sufficient strength to find an ever-fitting and never-failing agreement between what we call national consciousness and that which we regard as national feeling. The practical import of such unity is demonstrated by the Japanese nation. There being devout means at the same time being Japanese. From the correspondence between national and religious thought and feeling derives a patriotic force of tremendous dynamism. The best among us struggle towards this ultimate synthesis. Unfortunately we are not yet pledged in this religious way to our fallen heroes. Our historical tradition encumbers us with a thousand spiritual and mental inhibitions."

Would that the Führer might eventually be hailed as a god, chief among the deified dead who died for a nation that, instead of having the soul of a church (like the United States, in Chesterton's estimation), would be the Church. The 44-year-old Reich Minister of Propaganda was a poor Santa Claus: "Wandering through the mist, we feel in us and around us the hallowing and guiding force of our dead soldiers. With a thousand hands they draw us out of the anxiety of darkness and lead us towards the light of the coming day which awaits us."

There were enough dead to think about in the persistent Christmas season. The Russians began to take revenge on the Germans for the atrocities against civilians, executing many POWs and starving or overworking others. Of the more than three million prisoners taken by the Soviets, nearly half a million died in captivity. J. Edgar Hoover directed the FBI to start a file on Charlie Chaplin's efforts to persuade the Allies of the good will of Stalin and the Soviet system. Nine days before Christmas, Hitler ordered the extermination of all Gypsies, and anyone with a trace of Gypsy blood was destined for "resettlement camps" – which, more often than not, meant Auschwitz. On the same day, an envoy of Mussolini urged upon Hitler an accommodation, even a peace agreement, with the Russians, for the Duce had decided that a double-front war could not be won. Soviet troops had overwhelmed the Italian forces 100 miles north of Stalingrad. Hitler had forbidden any retreat by German soldiers, but they were spread thin with little reserves along the southern front in Russia.

While Goebbels celebrated the assassination of Admiral François Darlan in North Africa, after the Vichy admiral had declared that French ships in Mediterranean ports would be at the disposal of the Allies, Enrico Fermi and his team initiated a self-sustaining nuclear reaction at the University of Chicago. Three days after Christmas, Franklin Roosevelt forbade the Los Alamos scientists to share atomic secrets with the British, while he kept closely informed of the British advance into Burma to drive out the Japanese, begun on December 21.

Vatican Radio was more than an irritant to Goebbels, who saw to it that any German citizen caught listening to it could be convicted of a capital offense. It had been under the direction of the Society of Jesus, making the Jesuit general Father Wlodimir Ledóchowski, its de facto director. As a Pole animated in patriotic sentiment, Father Ledóchowski often was frustrated by the Pope's insistence on strict conformity to the provisions of the Lateran Treaty forbidding any condemnation of specific nations or leaders by the Holy See. Ledóchowski had worked closely with one of the French broadcasters, the Belgian priest Emmanuel Mistiaen, who was deprived of a keen advocate by the death of the Pole who shared his strong anti-Fascism. Mistiaen would resign in March 1943, in protest against new restrictions requiring that he submit transcripts to a censor before transmission. When the Pope became aware of this new policy, he refused Mistiaen's resignation, urging him to continue his subtle but consistent pro-Allied reporting, and replaced the censor. While the probity of the Pope's meticulous conformity to protocol is debated in retrospect, it frustrated Goebbels more than the staff of Vatican Radio by making it difficult for him to caricature the Vatican's broadcasting as a raucous propaganda megaphone. Mindful of the failed strategies of Pope Leo X with the German princes and Pope Pius V with Elizabeth I, but more cognizant of the retaliatory strategies by the Nazis on an horrific modern scale, Pope Pius XII avoided naming names and condemned evil in terms as generic as the Ten Commandments. A condensed version of the 7,0000-word *Opus Justitiae Pax* took the Holy Father 40 minutes to broadcast on Christmas Eve. The title (from Isaiah 32:17) was his personal motto, which he had taken from a wall inscription in the piazza of Santa Maria della Pace where he had played as a child. The *New York Times* editorial on Christmas Day passed its pro-life judgment on the Pope, whose divisions were not contained by time and space:

> "This Christmas more than ever he is a lonely voice crying out of the silence of a continent. Pope Pius expresses as passionately as any leader on our side the war aims of the struggle for freedom when he says that those who aim at building a new world must fight for free choice of government and religious order. They must refuse that the state should make of individuals a herd of whom the state disposes as if they were lifeless things."

The Pope's critique of statism was clear without even having to read between the lines:

"After the fatal economy of the past decades, during which the lives of all citizens were subordinated to the stimulus of gain, there now succeeds another and no less fateful policy, which, while it considers everybody and everything with reference to the State, excludes all thought of ethics or religion. This is a fatal error. It is calculated to bring about incalculable consequences for social life, which is never nearer to losing its noblest prerogatives than when it thinks it can deny or forget with impunity the eternal Source of its own dignity, which is God."

Opposition to this oppression by the secular state was to be a crusade, with the *"Deus lo vult!"* cry of Godfrey of Bouillon:

"It is for the best and most distinguished members of the Christian family, filled with the enthusiasm of crusaders, to unite in a spirit of truth, justice and love to the cause. God wills it! Ready to serve, to sacrifice themselves, like the crusaders of old! If the issue was then the liberation of a land hallowed by the life of the incarnate Word of God, the call today is, if We may so express Ourselves, to traverse the sea of errors of our day, and to march on to free the holy land of the spirit which is destined to sustain in its foundation the unchangeable norms and laws on which would arise a social construction of sound internal consistency."

The crusade for human dignity would entail a defense of the indissolubility of marriage and the primacy of the family in educating children:

"The bond of trust and mutual help should be re-established between the family and the public school; that bond which in other times gave such happy results, but which now has been replaced by mistrust where the school, influenced and controlled by the

spirit of materialism, corrupts and destroys what the
parents have instilled into the minds of the children."

The Pope detailed how the subversion of marriage and the family went in tandem with the manipulation of the juridical order.
"The juridical sense of today is often altered and overturned by
the expression and the practice of a positivism and utilitarianism
which are subjected and bound to the service of determined
groups; classes and movements whose programs direct and
determine the course of legislation and the practices of the
courts." The integrity of law required "clear juridical norms
which may not be overturned by unwarranted appeals to the
supposed popular sentiment, or by merely utilitarian considera-
tions." Belgian magistrates understood this as an endorsement
of their stop-work protest against the imposition of Nazi law on
their courts. They had declared illegal the decrees of Gerard
Romsée, a quisling secretary-general of the Ministry of the
Interior who had used the murder of the Rexist burgomaster of
Charleroi as an excuse to create a civil police force under the
Office of the Interior, removed from the jurisdiction of the public prosecutor. The magistrates' protest and the Pope's message
only inflamed the Germans and the new police force expedited
the deportation of Belgian Jews.

It was for the local bishops to apply the guidelines of the
Pope's social analysis to their immediate circumstances.
Anticipating the Allied landings in French North Africa,
Archbishop Charles-Albert Gounot did just that when he
denounced the persecution of the Jews by the Vichy government. The archbishop of Carthage – in the venerable tradition of
the first bishop of Carthage, Epaentus, a convert of Achaia, and
the sixth bishop, St. Cyprian, martyred in the Valerian persecution in 258 – had already earned his credentials as an opponent
of Vichy attempts virtually to suborn the bishops. Archbishop
Gounot also indicted the pro-Mussolini Italian residents of
Tunisia who "foment discord."

French Catholicism was not totally absorbed in the political agonies of the day. At least there was sober gratitude for the final authentication of a miracle at Lourdes: that of Mlle. Joséphine Chabon, who, during a 1941 pilgrimage, had been saved from the amputation of a shattered foot, which had been instantaneously healed. And in other realms of the Spirit, the Holy See announced plans to beatify Marie-Clotilde of Savoy, daughter of Victor-Emmanuel II. She had suffered a miserable marriage to the son of King Jerome, cousin of Napoleon III, and evidenced heroic virtue in the Third Order of St. Dominic, which she joined in 1871 with the name of Marie-Catherine of the Sacred Heart. The cause of Mother Frances Cabrini was advancing. The foundress of the Missionary Sisters of the Sacred Heart had died in 1917. The Holy See also encouraged those promoting the cause of Charles de Foucauld. His works among the Tuaregs of the Sahara were considered of timely significance for the events unfolding in North Africa. Ironically, his martyrdom in 1916 outside his compound in Tamanrasset in southern Algeria by marauders connected with the Senussi Bedouins would delay honors of the altar out of post-war concerns for Muslim relations. He would be beatified in 2005, seven months after the election of Pope Benedict XVI.

The Axis powers had organized a Youth Congress in September in Vienna. The Vatican took note that only the Spanish delegation sang Catholic songs "in an atmosphere charged with Nationalist-Socialist neo-paganism." Receiving the credentials of the new Spanish ambassador to the Holy See, Señor Domingo de las Bárcenas y Lopez-Mollinedo, before Christmas, the Pope said, "At this culminating point in the history of the world, Spain has beyond doubt a lofty mission to fulfill: she will be worthy of it if she succeeds in finding herself again completely with her traditional Christian spirit, and with the unity which can only be built upon the spirit."

When the Atlantic Ocean was not yet a pond, 5,000 semi-hysterical bobby-soxers in New York City attended another kind of youth rally at the New Year's Eve debut of Frank Sinatra at the Paramount Theater. He was introduced by Jack Benny as an "extra added attraction." Some in the crowd began to faint, and the deafening screams frightened the official star, Benny Goodman, who turned to the audience and said, "What the hell is that?" But the ocean was not that vast, and in due time some of those in the audience would be receiving telegrams on behalf of the Secretary of War with names of fathers and brothers.

13. Lamentations

On the first day of the new year, in anticipation of his declaration of "Total War" twelve days later, Adolf Hitler had decided to make better use of manpower, weapons, and armor-plating by scrapping the High Seas Fleet. On January 3, Canadian troops landed in North Africa, one week before the Soviet Red Army entered Stalingrad. On January 14, the day after U.S. troops captured Galloping Horse Ridge on Guadalcanal, Winston Churchill and Franklin Roosevelt began their eleven-day-long meeting at Casablanca. While attention was directed at the Soviet success in breaking the German siege of Leningrad on January 18, the Jews of the Warsaw Ghetto rose up in resistance.

The ghetto had been designated such on October 16, 1940, by the German Governor-General Hans Frank, isolated with barbed wire, and contained about 30 percent of the population of Warsaw, or about 400,000 Jews. On January 18, the people of the ghetto were ordered to assemble for documentation. According to plans of Heinrich Himmler, who had visited Warsaw on January 9, 8,000 were to be deported to the Treblinka concentration camp. Between July 23 and September 21 (Yom Kippur) in 1942, after more than 100,000 had died of starvation and disease, more than 254,000 had been sent to die at Treblinka. This time they hid rather than comply. Among the thousand or so who were captured, some of the group who were armed with pistols, led by Mordechai Anielewicz, engaged the German guards in hand-to-hand fighting. The German troops withdrew after four days, having met only about 10 percent of their quota for Treblinka.

"Judah has gone into exile because of affliction and hard servitude; she dwells now among the nations, but finds no resting place; her pursuers have all overtaken her in the midst of her distress." (Lam 1:3) Several thousand German troops would enter the ghetto under the command of Jürgen Stroop on the eve of Passover, April 19, leveling the whole area and killing or deporting 56,065 Jews and, on May 16, blowing up the Great Synagogue of Warsaw. Stroop later remembered: "What a wonderful sight! I called out, Heil Hitler! and pressed the button. A terrific explosion brought flames right up to the clouds. The colors were unbelievable. An unforgettable allegory of the triumph over Jewry." *Gruppenführer* Stroop was executed on March 6, 1952.

As the Axis increasingly fought a defensive battle, possibly hoping at best for a stalemate, large segments of the Italian populace became restless about their prospects, while German propaganda assured them that they would get their share of the *Lebensraum*. The editor of the *Giornale degli Economisti*, Giovanni de Maria, wrote: "It is improbable that any people would accept such open vassaldom, which infringes not only the principle of human freedom, but also the desire of every people to develop according to its own capacities, without foreign guidance."

In 1926, Pope Pius XI had sent the Jesuit priest Rev. Joseph Ledit of the Oriental Institute in Rome to investigate religious conditions in the Soviet Union. In an interview in November 1942 and translated into English shortly after Christmas, he had estimated that, as of the outbreak of the war, there was only one Catholic priest ministering freely there. Of the Catholic priests ordained in Russia before its revolution, about 150 were confined to Soviet gulags. Seventy Polish priests, deported in 1939, were recently released to serve in the conquered Polish forces, and eleven were given charge of millions of Polish Catholics. The Polish Field Bishop, Msgr. Józef Gawlina, said that "their activities are of a purely private character, since they cannot hold public church ceremonies." The New York Society for the Propagation of the Faith was undaunted, and cheerfully reported "an encouraging growth of fervor" among Russian Catholics in Shanghai where a newly ordained priest of the Byzantine rite and American sisters of St. Columban were establishing a school for ethnic Russian boys in China who would provide vocations to "rebuild the now decimated Catholic clergy of Russia."

By the beginning of 1943, the quisling premier of the Nazi puppet state of Croatia had created a schismatic church for the Orthodox. In Belgium, the Germans forbade Jozef-Ernest Cardinal van Roey to publish Pius XII's silver jubilee address, and the Italian government banned from all Italian cinemas the film *Pastor Angelicus*, about the life of the Pope.

An English translation of the last 28 sermons preached in the Berlin suburb of Dahlem by the Lutheran pastor Martin Niemöller before his arrest was published under the title *The Gestapo Defied*. Niemöller had tentatively supported Hitler years before:

> "It is true that Hitler betrayed me. I had an audience with him, as a representative of the Protestant Church, shortly before he became Chancellor, in 1932. Hitler promised me on his word of honor, to protect the Church, and not to issue any anti-Church laws. He also agreed not to allow pogroms against the Jews, assuring me as follows: 'There will be restrictions against the Jews, but there will be no ghettos, no pogroms, in Germany.'"

Niemöller spent the years 1938 to 1945 in the Sachsenhausen and Dachau concentration camps. Hitler did not arrest the German Catholic bishops, as he did Niemöller, out of political pragmatism. The Archbishop of Canterbury, Dr. William Temple, who would die October 26, 1944, spoke in January 1943 in a German Lutheran Church in London in tribute to Pastor Niemöller. He also cited the protests of the bishops of Münster and other Roman Catholic bishops "against the closing of religious houses throughout Germany." He added that the Christians of Holland and France, "at great risk to themselves and their Churches, have condemned the treatment of the Jews, but not so far as we have heard, the Christians of Germany." He failed to cite the declarations of Michael Cardinal von Faulhaber and Bishop Clemens August Graf von Galen.

On January 23, a Catholic commentator wrote in London's *Tablet* on the tendency to think that more would have been accomplished by a louder protest by some prelates:

> "If there exists a vague atavistic memory that once Popes and Bishops spoke, and wicked Kings trembled, that salutary thing happened because the public opinion of the day had a much fuller and deeper sense of the rights and importance of spiritual authority. Modern men, who have for so long applauded the narrowing down and emptying of that authority as the emancipation of mankind from the thralldom of superstition, can hardly be surprised if, as a rule, prelates in the modern era tend in prudence to limit themselves to the field indubitably conceded to them by public opinion."

On that same January 23, U.S. forces seized control of Japan's last two strongholds on Guadalcanal, the U.S.S. *Guardfish* sank the Japanese destroyer Kakaze, and the Casablanca Conference ended. So it was agreed to invade Sicily and also make an assault across the English Channel on Western Europe.

As the Anglo leaders were packing up their briefcases, the Eighth Army in Libya was advancing on Tripoli. In the 18th century, Tripoli (along with the other Barbary Coast lands of Tunis, Morocco, and Algiers) had challenged our own new republic's diplomacy by their piracy. Thomas Jefferson and John Adams met in London in March 1786 with Sidi Haji Abdul Rahman Adja, the representative of the Dey of Algiers to Britain. Their question posed was why the Muslims were hostile to the new United States, which had done no harm to the Muslim people. The Dey's response, as reported to the Congress, was that "Islam was founded on the Laws of their Prophet, that it was written in their Quran, that all nations who should not have acknowledged their authority were sinners, that it was their right and duty to make war upon them wherever they could be found, and to make slaves of all they could take as Prisoners, and that every Musselman who should be slain in Battle was sure to go to Paradise."

Congress favored appeasement, by bribing the pirates in the form of annual tribute. Jefferson objected but Adams approved, saying: "We ought not to fight them at all unless we determine to fight them forever." As soon as Jefferson became president, and Tripoli broke its truce, the Tripolitan War began, though not formally declared by Congress. In 1943, those at Casablanca were too occupied with the moment to remember that earlier war, but today it does not seem long ago at all, and not without present application.

14. Light the Candles

In the House of Commons in the last week of January, a Labour member for North-West Camberwell, Charles Ammon, spoke in favor of bombing Rome. He was a lifelong Socialist and Methodist lay preacher who would be raised to the peerage the following year as 1st Baron Ammon of Camberwell and then serve as chief whip in the House of Lords. His insistence that this be an essential part of the Allied offensive was supported by Sir Archibald Southby, a Conservative for Epsom, and also by Eleanor Rathbone, an independent member for the Combined English Universities.

In his first speech, Ammon argued for bombing Rome from points of military strategy. Having been unsatisfied with the ambiguous replies of the foreign secretary, he appealed again by asking why the Vatican had not been more outspoken in condemning Nazi atrocities. The foreign secretary spoke of the numerous times the Vatican had done so. *The Tablet* commented that the questioners "afforded one more example of the anxiety of the ordinary Englishman, whenever he feels strongly about a matter, to have the Pope on his side – an anxiety matched only by his rage when a Papal pronouncement is made from which he happens to differ."

The Vatican continued to broadcast the New Year message of Archbishop Josef Frings of Cologne, which contained among its many grievances against the German government a protest more mordant than plaintive: "The clergy are no longer allowed to give religious instruction in the elementary schools, and religious instruction has been reduced to a minimum, if not cut altogether." Archbishop Frings announced the establishment of

"Hours of Spiritual Instruction" (*Seelsorgestunden*) twice weekly for all Catholic schoolchildren in defiance of the government. This would accommodate children wherever they might be, as many were being evacuated from one district to another. "It is the parents' duty to see that the children learn the truth, the more so since everything is done on the other side to imbue our children with an un-Christian spirit and to prejudice them against the Church of Christ."

The Vatican Polyglot Press produced in book form the articles of Professor Guido Gonella, an editor of *L'Osservatore Romano*, on *The Essential Conditions of International Order*. This exercised the easily outraged *Critica Fascista*, which complained that once again the Church was showing herself to be "obsolete" and "medieval" and was "thinking of a return to the days of Dante." Gonella, fumed the Fascist journal, had wrongly confused Hegel's State-worship with the Fascist state. "We should like it expressly stated that what the Church has to say is of a religious nature: the ambiguous term 'morality' should not be used, for it can hide conceptions of other days, when the State had to attend only to material interests, and everything else was a matter for the Church."

Giving special publicity to an item from the *Neue Zurcher Zeitung* of December 29, 1942, which said that in the previous autumn Pope Pius XII had discussed "social questions" with President Roosevelt's personal representative to the Holy See, the Vatican Radio added with flamboyant paralipsis: "We are not in a position to confirm these statements by the Swiss paper, as up to the present complete silence has been maintained by both sides on the discussions."

The archbishop of Milan, Alfredo Ildefonso Cardinal Schuster, sent to all his parishes a pastoral letter in response to Fascist propaganda against the Holy See. "Pius XII, remaining absolutely outside and above – much above – all the interests that inspire the various armies, took to himself the part of a common father to sorrowing humanity." Cardinal Schuster had been impressed by Mussolini's role in the Lateran Treaty and was the first bishop to take an oath of loyalty to the Italian state in 1929, in the presence of King Victor Emmanuel III, according to the protocols of the pact. This was a few weeks before he was created a cardinal. Cardinal Schuster enthusiastically endorsed the Ethiopian campaign in 1935, declaiming that it would provide a vast area for missions promoting "the Catholic faith and Roman civilization." After the deaths of 750,000 native Abyssinians, sometimes by chemical warfare, his measure of Mussolini changed. On April 25, 1945, he would invite the Duce to the episcopal palace in Milan and, over a glass of wine, instruct him in the need for humility and the timeliness for being reconciled with God. Mussolini finished his wine and left; three days later, he was assassinated.

Schuster had in fact openly opposed Mussolini since 1938 in response to the anti-Jewish laws of the Fascists. In a sermon on November 13 he preached: "A kind of heresy has emerged abroad and is infiltrating more or less everywhere, which not only attacks the supernatural foundations of the Catholic Church, but . . . denies humanity any other spiritual value, and thus constitutes an international danger no less serious than that of Bolshevism itself. It is what is called racism." The Fascists strongly objected to Schuster's words but he was supported by Pius XI who sent a message: "The Holy Father exhorts the cardinal of Milan to uphold Catholic doctrine courageously, because this point cannot be ceded. . . ."

Many principled non-Fascists admired the early Mussolini and later turned against him, including Pius XI. Cardinal Vanutelli said Mussolini "had been chosen to save the nation and restore her fortune." Mussolini allied with the Nazis only after Pius XI declined to excommunicate Hitler publicly, as Mussolini had wanted in order to weaken Hitler's influence in Austria. Franklin Roosevelt had once called Mussolini "that admirable Italian gentleman" and later based parts of his National Recovery Administration on some of Mussolini's structures. In judgments of character, the fine line in him between optimist and naif was often trespassed. Even later, as late as

February 1945 when he returned from the Yalta Conference, Roosevelt told members of his cabinet: "I think that something entered into Stalin's nature of the way in which a Christian gentleman should behave." Churchill at first thought Mussolini was a "Roman genius . . . the greatest lawgiver among men." In 1927 he wrote: "If I had been an Italian I am sure that I should have been whole-heartedly with you from the start to finish in your triumphant struggle against the bestial appetite and passions of Leninism." As early as 1925, G. K. Chesterton admiringly, but mistakenly, attributed to Mussolini the line: "If I advance; follow me! If I retreat; kill me! If I die; avenge me!" The words were those of Henri de la Rochejaquelein, leader of the Vendean insurrection against the French revolutionaries in 1793, and Chesterton doubtless would have approved them even more had he known that. His book "The Resurrection of Rome" admires Mussolini's achievement. In 1930 he had private audiences with Pius XI and Mussolini and found the latter especially fascinating, and believed Mussolini when he said that he had read many of his guest's books. In a most unlikely exchange, obviously choreographed by Mussolini to avoid uncomfortable topics, Chesterton and the Duce discussed in French the revision of the Anglican Book of Common Prayer. While trying to make sense of Fascism, the Englishman warned that it "appeals to an appetite for authority, without giving the authority for the appetite."

On March 8, 1945, Allen Dulles, as head of the U.S. Office of Strategic Services, would meet in Lucerne with *Obergruppenführer* and General of the Waffen-SS Karl Wolff, who was then Military Plenipotentiary for Italy, to work out a secret surrender of German troops in Italy. Under interrogation as a prisoner in May 1945, Wolff testified that Cardinal Schuster had been consulted in the surrender plans and had urged that Mussolini not be included, for he suspected that, even at that late stage, Mussolini would block the surrender. At Nuremburg, Wolff was spared execution because of his cooperation, and he died in 1984. The future Pope John XXIII sang Cardinal Schuster's

Requiem Mass in 1954, and three years later the future Pope Paul VI opened the diocesan process for his canonization. In 1996, Pope John Paul II beatified Cardinal Schuster, whose remains were incorrupt when exhumed in 1985. Some saints have made big mistakes in politics and even in private revelations. Their sanctity is based on heroic virtue and the state of their souls at death.

At the start of 1943, there were only about 4,000 Catholics in Sweden. Episcopal statements often took the form of public correspondence with the Lutheran bishops. The vicar apostolic, Msgr. Johannes Muller, had ordered that the Fourth Sunday of Advent be kept by Catholics as a day of prayer for "all those who are unjustly persecuted, oppressed and tortured, and the Jews in particular." He then published a letter to the Lutheran Archbishop Erling Eidem: "It fills our hearts with acute pain and horror to know that all over Europe people are persecuted, tortured, killed or mercilessly driven from home and country merely because they belong to a certain race or have defended the freedom of their country and ancient rights inherited from their fathers."

In this January 1943 in Norway, where the Catholic population was no more than 3,000, according to reports sent to the Stockholm *Dagens Nyheter*, the Gestapo arrested two parish priests, the Taxt brothers, of Oslo and Bergen. A third, Father van der Vlugt of Hamar, was sent to Germany and not heard from again. On January 17, the Nazi newspaper in Denmark, *Kritisk Ugerevue*, attacked Bishop Johannes Theodor Suhr because it was his policy to refuse a Requiem Mass for any Dane who had joined the German forces. Moreover, the Catholic Church in Denmark "prays for Hitler's death and Germany's destruction."

In the last week of January, the Allies captured Tripoli and the first all-American air raid was launched on Germany, with 50 bombers. The Japanese had abandoned the Papua campaign, while continuing to fight in western Guadalcanal, though on January 30 they completely evacuated, undetected by the Americans. Near Guadalcanal, Americans were defeated by the

Japanese in the naval battle of Rennel Island. The United States XIV Corps arrived in the Pacific Theater; while back in Europe, on January 31, the newly minted Field Marshal Friedrich Paulus and more than 90,000 German troops of the German 6th Army surrendered to the Soviets at Stalingrad. Then began a fast march to Rostov and the Kerch Peninsula to rescue the Armies of the Caucasus. Hitler's own amateurish hand, disdaining advice, had brought havoc before Moscow in 1941 and on the Volga in 1942. Anxiety among his top commanders was increasing with a foreboding made worse by its silence.

In England, where dark austerity was beginning to lighten a little, Mary G. Chadwick published a poem, "For Our Lady in War-Time," to mark the approaching liturgical feast of February 2. She wrote it unaware that, on the feast, the German 6th Army would officially surrender at Stalingrad. For the first time in the war, the Germans publicly acknowledged a defeat and ordered three days of mourning.

> Light the candles at dawn of day;
> Light eternal in flames that pass
> Burn in the Church and burn in the choir,
> Set the altar for Candlemas.
>
> Here is incense grey as the dawn,
> Holy water and holy fire,
> Bless the candles and hold them up . . .
> Light of the World and the World's Desire!
>
> Carry them home as treasure trove,
> The Church has blessed and the Church has prayed,
> Danger of body and hurt of soul
> By her holy praying be swift delayed.
>
> Crash of bombs and roar of the guns,
> Pain and terror and death upstart,
> Like a frightened child in a world of ill
> Hide your face on our Lady's heart!

Light the candles when night is black,
Light eternal in flames that pass,
Pure gold fire upon purest wax –
Light the candles of Candlemas.

15. Progressive Evil

"The Judgment of the Nations" was a work published in 1942 by the Catholic historian, Christopher Dawson, but it started to get significant attention only in the early months of 1943. "The old landmarks of good and evil and truth and falsehood have been swept away and civilization is driving before the storm of destruction like a dismasted and helmless ship." Dawson saw around him countless proofs that "evil too is a progressive force and that the modern world provides unlimited prospects for its development." Things spiritual had been invaded by the secular State with a resulting fragmentation of Christendom which "while it is not the end of Christianity, is in point of fact the fruit of Christianity." A secular substitute for the unifying power of Christendom had been attempted in the League of Nations, but it was "a juridical skeleton of international order and no more." In the vacuum rose the totalitarian State which imposed "total control of all human activities and all human energies, spiritual as well as physical…and their direction to whatever ends are dictated by its interests, or rather the interests of the ruling party or clique."

On the same day, February 2, that the Battle of Stalingrad ended, Rommel continued his retreat into Tunisia, and within a few days the Allies had full control of Libya and simultaneously began a four-month lone attack on the Ruhr industrial region. The British under General Wingate advanced into Burma on February 8 and the Americans secured Guadalcanal the next day, as Munich, Vienna and Berlin were being bombed. General Eisenhower was given command of the Allied armies in Europe on the 11th and two days later Rommel took Sidi bouzid and

Gafsa in western Tunisia and began the Battle of the Kasserine Pass. Newly arrived American troops were forced into retreat, sending shock waves across the United States, where the costs of war were taking their toll on the most basic levels: even shoes began to be rationed.

Far more dire were the consequences of deprivation in Europe. The Belgian Ministry of Economic Affairs announced that tuberculosis had increased more than 20 percent in just six months, due to undernourishment. Ten million French people were suffering from hunger, having lost an estimated 200 million kilograms in weight since the start of the war. Expectant mothers were receiving just one-half their normal food rations. In Paris, cases of scabies increased by 70 percent and the German authorities requisitioned as many as 3,000 available hospital beds for their own use, while virtually eliminating all ambulances. The birth rate had declined to 600,000 from 780,000 ten years earlier and it was predicted that if such a rate of decline continued, the population of France by 1992 would be only 30 million. The decline did not continue, and in 1992 the population was about 57 million, increasing to 65 million in 2010, but this was significantly inflated by immigration. Medical authorities in Greece feared the loss of a whole generation of youth, and in Norway people were fainting in the food queues and factories due to under-nourishment. One health report anticipated the death of ten per cent of the population by the end of the winter of 1943. By contrast, Dr. Conti, the Reich Medical Leader, boasted in the *Berliner Boersen Zeitung* that "the German people are very healthy.' He was embarrassed by statistics in the *Reichgesundheitsblatt* showing regular and dramatic increases in rates of diphtheria and virtually all other ailments. In pre-war Germany there was one doctor for about every 2,000 Germans, but by 1943 there was one doctor for every15,000.

February saw the English publication of the full text of the December 12, 1942, pastoral letter of the Bishop of Berlin, Johann Konrad Maria Augustine Felix Graf von Preysing Lichteness-Moos. When the Nazis had first come into power, he said, "We have fallen into the hands of criminals and fools." Bishop von Preysing's Advent message was not an uncertain trumpet: ". . . every departure from right and justice will sooner or later be broken against these foundations of God's Dominion." The world's present miseries were the result of human contempt for natural and divine law: "Resistance to God's sovereign rule was a product largely of the eighteenth century – the century which proclaimed the primacy of human intelligence, the individual as an autonomous being and as his own sole judge, and which declared that all right was to be derived from this intelligence independently of God's law." The State had imposed itself as the very incarnation of God, replacing justice and right with power and profit. There followed an obvious citation of Nietzsche: "A certain German philosopher who has been guiding the minds of a great many people, has exerted a harmful influence over the German nation by proclaiming that as far as specially endowed individuals and highly gifted nations are concerned, there can be no good or evil, no right or wrong; and that these are dispensed from respecting any questions of right or morality; that it is their privilege to deprive weaker nations or peoples of lower cultural level than themselves, or races which really or seemingly do not enjoy as any advantages, of every right." The bishop's appeal was stark: "My dear Brethren: 'Repent,' and change your mode of thinking. This is my appeal to you." His assistant, Father Bernard Lichtenberg, died en route to Dachau. Pope John Paul II beatified him in 1996.

On February 3, the day after Candlemass, a twenty-nine-year-old priest was ill with typhoid in Dachau, He requested Communion and was given a lethal injection. One of the prison guards said, "Christ does he want? A syringe he gets." Father Alois Andritzki was born in Dresden and had been a constant opponent of the Nazis, who imprisoned him in 1941 after he spoke out against the eugenics policies in the Saxonian sanitarium in Pima. Before the end of the war, about 16,000 patients, disabled or mentally ill, were killed as "life unworthy of life." His spiritual writings on the Passion of Christ had attracted many and continued to spread after his death. On June 13, 2011, in the Dresden Cathedral, he was beatified as a martyr at the direction of Pope Benedict XVI.

The pro-Nazi newspaper *Vooruit* of Ghent rued the pastoral letter of Cardinal van Roey who opposed forced labor. At the same time, the Primate of Hungary, Cardinal Serédi, told representatives of the Hungarian Catholic Press that "all States have equal sovereignty" and so "the Hungarian nation has a birthright to claim – freedom, autonomy, and national independence." The Vatican put to rest rumors that Benedetto Croce had been reconciled to the Church. In an article in his review "La Critica," Croce had spoken of the imperishable values of Christianity and the importance of the Church for human civilization, but had also maintained his view that the Church "had cramped the spirit by her dogmas." In Poland, the Germans suppressed all patriotic hymns, litanies and prayers and took particular umbrage at the practice of hailing the Virgin Mary as "Queen of the Crown of Poland." Dr. Mutz, Chief of the Department of Internal Administration, abolished all mentions of the Polish State "which no longer exists." May 3rd would no longer be celebrated as the day of the "Beatae Mariae Virginis Patronae Rei Publicae Poloniae." The August 15 "Actio gratiarum pro Victoria super Bolshevicos 1920" was forbidden, along with the thanksgiving for the victory at Chocim on October 10 and all services on November 11 commemorating the rebirth of the Polish Republic.

Father R. H. W. Regout, S.J., Professor of International Law at the Catholic University of Nijmegen, died at the age of 46 in Dachau, where he and three other professors had been sent shortly after the occupation of the Netherlands. The "Priestblock" in that concentration camp held 2579 priests over the war years, 1785 of them Polish, and only 816 are known to have survived. Twenty per cent of all the clergy in Poland died in the war. By February, 34 Italian chaplains had been killed on active service. The Archbishop of Reggio di Calabria, Msgr. Montalbetti, and his Chancellor, Msgr. Tarpini, were killed during an air raid at Melito Portosalvo. Cardinal Lavitrano, Archbishop of Palermo, which General Patton called the most conquered city in history, was injured and the Badia della Magione was destroyed. It had been built in the twelfth century for the Cistercians and was later used by the Teutonic knights. Lavitrano was not unaccustomed to calamity: as a boy in 1883 his entire family had been killed in an earthquake on the island of Ischia. He was respected by Pope Pius XII for trying to renew the piety of his people. In 1940 he had regretted that only 66 per cent of the Catholics of Palermo attended Mass on holy days, and only 12 per cent of the men made their Easter duties. The Pope did not find the situation in his own diocese of Rome much better. In 1945 Lavitrano become Prefect of the Sacred Congregation for Religious and died in 1950.

As appeals increasingly were being made to the Pope for help and advocacy in the war's distress, *L'Osservatore Romano* published an article on the history of papal diplomatic prerogatives by General Francois de Castelnau, President of the French Federation National Catholique. He remarked the irony by which the European powers in the nineteenth century had treated to exclude the Pope from their deliberations, while turning to him in crises. Seemingly debilitated by the loss of the Papal States in 1870, the Papacy ironically took on a new prestige when its loss of temporal power gave it a grander kind of neutrality. In 1885, Bismarck, only ten years removed from the Kulturkampf, had asked the Pope to arbitrate between two nations, Spain and Germany, for the first time in three centuries. In 1890 the Pope was asked to mediate between Great Britain and Portugal a matter of navigation on the Zambesi. In 1890 President Cleveland desired a papal arbitration between Venezuela and Great Britain to define the frontier between Venezuela and Guiana, and five years later he asked Leo XIII to do the same for Haiti and Santo Domingo. In 1898 the Pope actually accepted an invitation from the Czar to attend the Peace Conference at the Hague. When the Italian government blocked this, the Pope wrote to Queen Wilhelmina that he had hoped to perform a work "for which, whether through the Divine Founder of the Church, whether in virtue of age-old traditions, he had a kind of special vocation, that of mediator of peace."

With the emergence of virtually atheistic totalitarianism and its contempt for the appeal to neutrality, this role of the Pontiff was more constrained. In February, the Ashkenazi Chief Rabbi of Palestine and former Chief Rabbi of Ireland (1921 to 1936), Dr. Yitzhak Halevi Herzog, published a statement saying that he had appealed to the Pope to intervene with the combatant powers on behalf of European Jewry. The Holy See had replied that "the Pope is doing everything in his power on behalf of the persecuted Jews of Europe." Rabbi Herzog remained as Chief Rabbi until 1959 and a son, Chaim Herzog, would become President of Israel. When World War II ended, Rabbi Herzog said, "The people of Israel will never forget what His Holiness and his illustrious delegates are doing for our unfortunate brothers and sisters in the most tragic hour of our history, which is living proof of Divine Providence in this world."

16. Grievances against the Holy See

During February, the Eighth Army realized that local German advances in Tunisia signaled that no jejeune horoscope could be trusted. Rommel's progress and the shock of the Battle of the Kasserine Pass were sobering to Allied forces, especially the newly minted American troops. The Nazis had a new dose of adrenalin, and Joseph Goebbels declared a "Total War" against the Allies five days later on February 18, the same day that members of the anti-Nazi youth group, the "White Rose" movement, were arrested.

Communist parties had been illegal through most of Europe before 1939. The Soviet Union gradually entered international politics as Germany withdrew into itself, and by 1941 Holland, Belgium, and Yugoslavia had diplomatic representatives in Moscow. Molotov's pact with Hitler in 1939 was as cynical as the Russian-German treaty of Rapallo had been in 1922. All that was now overthrown by the decision of Reich leaders to justify National Socialism in the eyes of the church as an anti-Bolshevik crusade. When Finland succumbed to that posture, its minister to the Holy See was recalled to Helsinki.

From the United States, Archbishop Francis Spellman kept in close communication with the Vatican Secretariat of State, which he had served as the first American attaché beginning in 1925. He had first met Eugenio Cardinal Pacelli, soon to be Pope Pius XII, on a mission in Germany in 1927. Archbishop Spellman's superior in Boston, the imperious William Cardinal O'Connell, looked down on his diminutive former auxiliary bishop in every way: Archbishop Spellman was "what you get when you teach a bookkeeper how to read." Pope Pius XII thought differently. In this month of February, after the first major American offensive in the Pacific war had secured Guadalcanal, Archbishop Spellman made a "social visit" to President Franklin Roosevelt before leaving for Rome. As Under-Secretary of the Navy during the First World War, Roosevelt had twice rejected Spellman's request to be exempted from the height requirement for a naval chaplaincy. Roosevelt now told the press that the archbishop was traveling on "ecclesiastical business, arising out of his connection with the American Forces as chaplain-in-chief."

The Soviets lost the Third Battle of Kharkov on February 16, and the Americans took the Russell Islands, part of the Solomon chain, five days later. In between, on February 17, Archbishop Spellman arrived in Barcelona and, for stated reasons of bad weather, did not proceed to Rome until three days later, where he was received by the Pope that evening, and again on February 21 and 22. While in Spain, the New York prelate had called on General Francisco Franco at the El Pardo Palace and the foreign minister, Count Jordana. He was accompanied by the U.S. ambassador, Carlton J. Hayes.

In Washington, Cordell Hull told the press that he did not know the reason for Archbishop Spellman's trip. The Vatican, confirming Roosevelt's explanation, said that he was visiting U.S. chaplains in Europe, as well as North Africa and England. According to the Lateran treaty, Italy had granted the right of passage only to regularly accredited Vatican diplomats and cardinals. The archbishop was not a diplomat and not yet a cardinal, and so the Italian government granted him passage as a "special courtesy." The Brooklyn *Eagle* wildly speculated that Archbishop Spellman was arranging the departure of the Pope for South America.

In these same February weeks, a Flemish-language broadcaster from Friesland, Ward Hermans, announced over the wireless in response to the Church's opposition to forced labor:

"Their Most Exalted and Most Revered Eminences the Bishops of Belgium recently issued a Pastoral Letter purporting to speak for all workers coming under the labor conscription who have left to work in Germany. They talk of distress, compulsion and the like. Now, there are large numbers of workers who came voluntarily, immediately after the capitulation, just to earn a decent living. They never had an encouragement from the Church, and still they came. . . . Perhaps those in high places knew nothing of the true conditions of the people, but when millions are writing truth in letters of blood, others, however exalted their station, have no right to lie, high up on their pinnacles."

In a similar vein, the Flemish journal *De SS Man* of February 6 wrote: "Whatever Flemish disease you examine, you always find that the rottenness of the Belgian school organization is the root of the trouble. . . . We mean the numerous schools belonging to all kinds of priests and padres and brothers and nuns, which are the fortresses of their politics." The same newspaper claimed that "every time they see a plane, the nuns at Melgesdreef school, at Merksem, say a lightning prayer that the Germans may crash to the ground."

In what used to be Occupied and Unoccupied France, Emmanuel Cardinal Suhard and Pierre-Marie Cardinal Gerlier presided over meetings of bishops in early February. Cardinal Suhard, having had two audiences with the Holy Father, wrote in a pastoral letter that the Pope was well aware of conditions in France. He expressed concern for French prisoners of war and for the clergy shortage, commending the extra-diocesan seminary at Lisieux, which was supplying priests to any part of the country. In the same week, Rev. Paul Doncoeur, S.J., the national French leader of the Catholic Boy Scouts Movement, was arrested by the Germans. Father Doncoeur had been a leader in the liturgical movement animated by the studies of Lambert Beauduin, Aime-Georges Martimort, Henri de Lubac, and Louis Bouyer. Father Doncoeur used the Boy Scouts as a laboratory for some of the attempts at liturgical renewal and lay evangelization. He survived arrest, dying in 1961. After the war, he was a technical consultant for the 1948 film *Joan of Arc* with Ingrid Bergman.

The *Journal de Genève* disclosed that in October the Vatican had received a list of complaints from Germany. First, National Socialist leaders had been offended that the Pope left Rome when Hitler visited. The last grievance was about the Catholic chaplains among the Polish troops in Russia. The complaints would cease and all would be "forgotten" if the Holy See would temper its ways.

The new "Physicians' Chamber" established in Holland was taking strides toward a comprehensive government health care plan under the direction of a board including Dr. K. Keijer, who wrote in *Het Nationale Dagblad*:

> "With that quiet self-confidence which emanates from our outlook on life, calmly but with the stubbornness we have acquired in the ten years' struggle for our world outlook, we shall take measures against anyone who impedes the National-Socialist medical program which we have formulated for the Netherlands. Nothing less than the health of our people is at stake, and in the future we shall tolerate no irresponsible experiments in this sphere. . . . Again, but now for the last time, I invite all those in the health services to co-operate, while I on my part am quite willing to over-look mistakes which they have made in the past."

In *Volk en Vaderland*, an annoyed correspondent signed P. C. Roo wrote: "The Roman Catholic and Protestant Churches have used the German idea of sterilization as a weapon to fight National-Socialism on theological grounds. They consider it unnatural and therefore unpermissible."

As the life of the mind perdures in its arts, whatever the circumstances, in *The Burlington Magazine* Dr. Jacob Hess gave his opinion that the statue in the church of S. Gregorio Magno on the Caelian Hill in front of the Palatine, long believed to be that of St. Gregory the Great, was Michelangelo's long-lost sculpture of

Pope Julius II. Michelangelo had not finished it, and it had been altered to represent St. Gregory by the French sculptor Nicolas Cordier, who died in 1612. Hess had fled Germany's anti-Semitic statutes for Rome in 1934, where a small grant from the Vatican Library enabled him to edit the *Vite* of Giovanni Baglione. Fleeing Italy in 1939, he continued his research in London at the Warburg Institute. Interned in Britain as a German in 1940, he returned after the war to Rome. Hess received reparations from the German government in 1950, and in 1953 a Deutsche *Forschungsgemeinschaft* funded his work. His house, the Villa Ostia, became a center for the study of baroque art until his death in 1969 at the age of 84.

Cordier, Hess maintained, had been free to revise the Michelangelo work because the scruples of the Counter-Reformation Curia had considered the Master somewhat less than respectable. Scruples were less demanding in Auschwitz, whose commandant, Asmus von Troschke, a notorious torturer, was appointed by the German high command as curator of the historical monuments of Cracow "for the sake of art and culture."

17. The Ides of March

The radical social commentaries of the United States vice-president, Henry Wallace, would lead to a tense exchange with Winston Churchill in May, but Wallace had already stirred controversy with his leftist reduction of international relations, and war itself, to an economic dialectic. As chairman of the Board of Economic Welfare in President Franklin D. Roosevelt's secret "war cabinet," he had offended the State Department by negotiating contracts with foreign countries. The commerce secretary, Jesse Jones, took umbrage when he tried to assume the purchasing authority of the Reconstruction Finance Corporation. Wallace accused Jones of delaying the shipment of quinine to dying Marines. With both Cordell Hull and Jones insulted, Roosevelt dissolved the Board of Economic Welfare in July.

Wallace's tours of Latin America in 1943 persuaded 13 of its countries to break relations with the Axis powers, but his own case was primarily against Fascism, which he sweepingly identified with capitalism. In March, he declared that the war was the result of poverty. Describing his own religious views as vaguely Buddhist, he found no place for sin and evil in his explanation of the causes of war and had little patience for contemplating the depth of what John Henry Cardinal Newman called "those giants, the passion and the pride of man." In *Leviathan*, Hobbes had said: "During the time men live without a common power to keep them all in awe, they are in that condition which is called war; and such a war, as is of every man, against every man." It is striking to realize that, replaced by Harry Truman on January 20, 1945, Wallace missed succeeding Roosevelt as president by eighty-two days.

When in March the Swiss government lifted the ban on the Communist Party, which had been imposed in 1940, the Germans cited it as proof that National Socialism was the only defense against creeping Bolshevism. Radio Bremen, broadcasting in Flemish, quoted Cardinal van Roey's condemnation of Marxism as if it were an approval of National Socialism: "By opposing, Bolshevism will simultaneously strike at all those elements whose aim is to enslave the whole of our population, the rich as well as the poor, the propertied as well as the working classes." Not mentioned was the Joint Pastoral Letter of the Belgian hierarchy in December, deploring the deportation of Belgian workers to Germany as slave labor.

No bishop had been more outspoken against all forms of totalitarianism than Arthur Cardinal Hinsley. His death on St. Patrick's Day was a somber loss for the Catholics of England. Prayers were also offered for him in Anglican cathedrals, and the Agudath Israel World Organization sent a message to the Apostolic Delegate: "We have seen so much evidence of brotherhood and loving-kindness from the Cardinal in these past years that we feel with all his other friends for his well-being."

Cardinal Hinsley was reared in Yorkshire, the son of a carpenter in the service of the 9th Lord Beaumont at Carlton Hall, which would be refashioned a decade later for the Catholic peer as Carlton Towers by Augustus Pugin's son Edward. The future cardinal studied at Ushaw and then at the Venerable English College in the flowering of the Thomistic revival during the pontificate of Pope Leo XIII. He returned to teach philosophy at Ushaw, founded a grammar school in Bradford, taught in the seminary at Wonersh in southern England, and spent twelve years as a parish priest until Pope Benedict XV appointed him rector of the English College in Rome in 1917, in which position he virtually refounded the college materially and spiritually. In 1928 he was named vicar apostolic in Africa, where he served for six years, coping with poor health, nearly dying from blackwater fever, a complication of falciparum malaria. Back in Rome, he settled in as a canon of St. Peter's, planning on a quiet retirement, until he was announced for Westminster in 1935.

The first year of his new office saw the start of civil war in Spain, for whose beleaguered churches he organized a relief committee. Although he assumed that his time at Westminster would be an interim post, within two years he was created a cardinal, which did not give him joy, and which especially surprised him since his outspoken opposition to the Italian government had made him many enemies, including some Italian cardinals who had taken offense at his opposition to the invasion of Abyssinia. He protested to Raffaele Cardinal Rossi that he was too old, but Pope Pius XI was sending a clear message and asked Hinsley to take as a motto the Pope's phrase, once used by St. Charles Borromeo, invoked at the canonization of John Fisher and Thomas More: *"tales ambio defensores"* – I surround myself with such defenders.

As cardinal, Hinsley voted in the conclave that elected Pope Pius XII, and the two had remained in close communication. His "Sword of the Spirit" campaign, to enlist all denominations against threats to democracy, gained wide support but also criticism for being too ecumenical. Churchill indicated both his regard for Cardinal Hinsley and his own vague ecclesiology when he privately wished that Hinsley might replace Dr. Lang, whom he considered an appeaser, as Archbishop of Canterbury in 1942. Lang said that Churchill "knows nothing about the Church, its life, its needs or its personnel." King George VI was deeply frustrated that protocol prevented him from attending the cardinal's funeral.

Coincident with the London funeral rites, which included the peripatetic Archbishop Francis Spellman fresh from Algiers, the British minister plenipotentiary to the Holy See, Sir D'Arcy Osborne, organized an elaborate Requiem Mass in St. Peter's for the English prelate, paid for by the British government. In his diary, he noted: "He was a great patriot, though perhaps more courageously outspoken regarding the Nazi persecution of the Church and other offences against the law of God and man than would please the hypersensitive neutrals of the Vatican. They probably do not realize how much he has done to counteract the unfavourable effects abroad of their neutrality."

In his panegyric preached at the requiem in London, the archbishop of Liverpool quoted lines of the late Pius XI: "For or against God. . . . This is the alternative that shall decide the destinies of all mankind. . . . Let all those who still believe in God and adore Him loyally and heartily, concur in order to ward off from mankind the great danger that threatens us all alike." The official German news agency issued its own communiqué: "Cardinal Hinsley, like the Archbishop of Canterbury, regards it as his supreme aim to further the spread of Bolshevism. As is well known, he recently issued a Pastoral Letter asking for daily prayers for the Soviets. Hinsley acquired world-wide notoriety for his violent hatred for the Germans, and for his campaigning for Bolshevism."

In his tribute to the cardinal, Rev. Jean Olphe-Galliard, chaplain to the Fighting French Forces, quoted from a speech of Charles de Gaulle in London in 1941:

> "For the feast of St. Joan of Arc which we spent in England, on the morrow of one of the worst of the air raids, and after the presentation of the Colours to units of the Fighting French Forces, under a sky glowing with the heat of the fires and gray with clouds of ash, the Archbishop received our Colours in his cathedral and blessed them."

The Germans were more approving of the president of the Slovak State, Msgr. Josef Tiso, who continued to minister as a parish priest while also being head of what had become since 1939 a German protectorate. Tiso had gone to Berlin, where he acquiesced to Hitler's ultimatum: Either Slovakia would declare its independence and then become a client of Germany, or Germany would permit Hungary and Poland to annex Slovakia after Germany had annexed the Czech territories of Czechoslovakia. It was, of course a posture: Poland had appropriated an area of the

Polish-Slovak border in 1939 with its majority Polish population following the Munich Agreement, and Hungary followed suit by absorbing border lands populated by Hungarians, according to the so-called Vienna Award. The stage was set, as Germany had planned, for the Slovak invasion of Poland with 50,000 troops in field divisions. Their losses were slight, as the Poles were principally engaged with the Germans. As a convinced Fascist and anti-Semite, in 1942 Tiso offered the Germans money to deport 60,000 Slovak Jews for extermination in Auschwitz, making Slovakia the only country to pay for such deportations.

On September 11, 1941, the Pope had officially protested against the introduction of racial laws. He instructed his chargé d'affaires to tell Tiso of "the profound distress of His Holiness for the sufferings to which so many persons are subjected against the laws of humanity and justice – because of their nationality or race. Let him know also that these injustices committed under his Government damage the prestige of his country and that the adversary exploits them to discredit the clergy and the Church in the whole world."

Deportation ceased for a while, and in March 1943, the auxiliary bishop of Budapest, Msgr. Endre Havas, gave Tiso a letter from Rome ordering him to stop all deportations of Jews under the threat that he would be excommunicated. Exactly one year earlier, the chargé, Msgr. Giuseppe Burzio, wrote: "It is not true that Jews deported would be sent to the service of work, the truth is that they are murdered." When in 1944 the Nazis called for "rail shipments of foreign workers" for Auschwitz, another papal intervention stopped it, but then the Germans directly intervened and ignored a further effort by the Holy See in August. The Pope sent Tiso a telegram saying that he was "greatly pained" by what was occurring. Tiso sent 13,500 more Jews to death camps, while the Pope arranged for 25,000 Jews to be hidden in monasteries.

At the time of Cardinal Hinsley's death, a false report of Tiso's death at Bratislava spread and was widely printed in the press. He survived the war, having destroyed 80 percent of the

Slovak Jews, and was hanged for collaboration and war crimes on April 18, 1947, wearing his clerical clothes on the gallows. The same day, he was buried secretly for fear that his grave would become a shrine for those Slovaks to whom he still was a hero.

The Dutch hierarchy issued a joint pastoral letter on Septuagesima Sunday, angering the Nazis. The socialist daily *Het Volk* editorialized: "Later on [the bishops] will cry out that this is religious persecution, but then we shall know that they have been removed from their places not because of their faith, but because of their lack of faith, as they wanted the Dutch people to conclude a Pact with Jewry." Then followed a sanguineous threat: "Churchmen and bad shepherds must disappear first. This is the demand of the moment, however difficult it may be to write of it and advocate it."

The archbishop of Palermo, Luigi Cardinal Lavitrano, wounded in an air raid, protested in *Avvenire* against "inhuman warfare," and he was joined by the archbishop of Genoa, Pietro Cardinal Boetto, who counted 72 churches damaged or destroyed in his archdiocese by Allied bombs, including the church of Santo Stefano where Columbus was baptized. Alessio Cardinal Ascalesi of Naples wrote: "There is no word strong enough to stigmatize so brutal an act, of which even savages would be ashamed." The British government conveyed to the Holy See an expression of regret for the death of the archbishop of Reggio di Calabria, Msgr. Enrico Montalbetti, killed in a bombing raid

The Vatican's response through *L'Osservatore Romano* to the passion of the Italian prelates was arch, if not disdainful:

> "These plaintive voices are understandable, but at the same time they bring to our minds the question, 'did these churches fulfill the mission for which they were built by past generations?' Where are today the crowds which once filled them? The sad truth is that the greater part of these fine churches have been left empty lately, or at the best have been filled only for

Sunday Mass, when the pleasure-hunting youth of the great cities kept their rendezvous in church. In these circumstances it should cause no surprise that the Lord, who permitted the destruction of the Temple of Jerusalem owing to the wickedness of the Jews, has now allowed bombs to fall on the churches deserted by the faithful."

18. Night Falls over Europe

German success in the Third Battle of Kharkov exasperated the Russians, although no one could foretell that it would be the last significant local German victory of the war. That was March 16, 1943, and the next day Stalin virtually demanded that the United States and Britain form a second European front to relieve the Red Army, which had been carrying the weight of the entire Eastern Front. Starting that same day, through the 19th of March, the Allies lost 21 merchant ships in attacks from nearly 40 U-boats. The Germans' recovery of breaches made by the Eighth Army in Tunisia tempered any Allied overconfidence there. A week earlier, Churchill had warned that planning for a post-war Europe would have to take second place to the goal of victory itself.

On the 18th of March, in a Lincolnesque gesture, the new leader of the Free French, General Henri Giraud, restored full property and full citizenship to French Jews. Prospects for Vichy France continued to fade when French Guiana renounced ties with Vichy and allied itself with the Free French.

The Vatican radio, broadcasting in German on March 22, repudiated Nazi claims that the late Cardinal Hinsley had prayed for Bolshevism on Red Army Day: "The Church does not condemn in any way the peoples of the Soviet Union in their entirety, for we bear them the most sincere and fatherly love. We only accuse the system." The message continued: "This high Prelate of the Church energetically took the part of those persecuted and deprived of their rights because of their nationality or origin. He thus acted as an advocate and defender of the rights of man so little respected today."

An assassination attempt on Hitler failed on March 20. Col. Rudolf von Gersdorff, chief of intelligence for General Gunther von Kluge, had planned to blow himself up along with Hitler by detonating a bomb with acid in the Zeughaus exhibit hall. Hitler left the hall too quickly, and Gersdorff repaired to the men's lavatory where he flushed the fuse down a toilet. In those same hours, the Nazis opened Crematorium IV at Auschwitz. This was a streamlined death machine with an underground gas chamber from which an elevator transported the corpses into the furnace.

The Belgian Ministry of Information issued a statement from London, where the Belgian government was in exile from 1940 to 1944, saying that the Germans had forged the statement supposedly written by Cardinal van Roey approving the Germans' "crusade" against Communism. This had rained criticism on the cardinal from many quarters, including the BBC. The false report had been broadcast only in Holland, and not in Cardinal van Roey's Belgium, in an effort to influence the Dutch clergy. The communiqué of the Minister of Information, Antoine Delfosse, stated:

> "In the highest Belgian quarters in London it is declared that the document referred to by the Hilversum Broadcasting Station is manifestly a gross forgery on the part of the enemy propagandists, designed to foment confusion in the minds of the public and to place the Archbishop in a delicate position, particularly in relation to a neighboring country, where the falseness of the supposed document cannot immediately be discovered."

In Belgium itself, the collaborationist journal *Cassandre* was outraged that in the diocese of Liege, February 8 had been designated a day of Prayer for the Jews. A parish magazine, *L'Appel des Cloches*, told the faithful: "In praying and going to Communion on that Sunday for the persecuted Jewish people, once the chosen people of Christ, we shall be acting in conformity with the instructions of our Right Reverend Bishop." The Belgian bishops prepared a second pastoral letter to be read in all the churches on the Second Sunday of Lent, saying that King Leopold, then a prisoner, and the Holy See joined them in condemning forced labor and deportations.

Priests in the French diocese of Mende, in Languedoc, were ordered by the diocesan chancellor not to give out information about church property, sacred vessels, or organizations. This was a precaution, given Nazi confiscation of church properties in Austria. In January 1943, the historic Göttweig monastery near Krems had been turned into a National Political Education Institute; and the Benedictine monastery of Echternach in Luxembourg, founded in 698 by St. Willibrord, was converted into schools of commerce and agriculture. From the Basilica in Fourvière in Lyons, Pierre-Marie Cardinal Gerlier preached a sermon in late February that began to circulate in Britain weeks later: "The worst of all catastrophes would be that the world, ravaged by what the Pope calls its 'progressive de-Christianization,' should continue to sink into paganism, which in several quarters, certain persons dream of substituting for the Christian ideal."

Marking the anniversary of the election of the Pope on March 2, the Vatican radio broadcast a special message in German: "Night has fallen over Europe. The demon of war has been unleashed and brings untold misery to peoples and nations, to States and families. Its presence is regarded as a licence for all imaginable cruelties. The persecution of religion, the suppression of monasteries and religious houses, the closing of churches and schools, an unexampled disregard of the dignities and rights of the human personality, an unprecedented enslavement of human freedom, the deportation of thousands for forced labour, the killing of innocent and guilty alike, the extermination of cultural values hundreds of years old, the thwarting of the humanities (*Verkuemmerung der Geitswissenschaften*), an unpardonable commandeering of human beings, especially of school and university youth, for the aims of a State that reigns supreme and has lost contact with the laws of

God. . . . The Pope sees all this and raises his warning voice of protest. Above all he suffers with the tortured people. His pains, however, are not of a depressing kind. They are the pains of one who is full of hope. The Pope is an optimist, not of the reactionary type, waiting for the return of past ages. He says: 'The watchword of the hour is not to bewail but to act.'"

Michael Cardinal von Faulhaber marked the papal anniversary preaching in the Munich cathedral:

> "The State, as an institution built by God, can establish its laws, and its subjects are under the obligation to obey them, for the sake of their conscience. The State has the right to levy taxes and to demand sacrifices of property and life in the defense of the Fatherland. The State, however, has no right to make laws which are incompatible with Divine Law and the Natural Law. . . . Thus, the meaning of family life does not lie exclusively in the building up of national strength."

Coincidentally, with unusual candor, the Gauleiter of the Office for Racial Policy, Kreisleiter Schneider, admitted that the German government's attempts to increase the birth rate of the *Herrenvolk* had failed, though he did not connect this with the Nazi hostility to the institution of the family. Marriages contracted between 1933 and 1939 had produced an average of less than two children, and 1942 had seen a more precipitous decline especially in the 63 largest towns: 342,000 births in 1942, in contrast to 395,600 in 1941. To German dismay, the Polish birth rate in urban areas "incorporated into the Reich" was 18.7 per thousand, as against 13.9 for Germans. To German dismay, the 1942 Polish figure had declined from 20.5 in 1940 largely due to German attempts at population control, but this was still unsatisfactory, and Arthur Greiser, Gauleiter of the Warthegau, was determined that more drastic steps had to be taken.

The British 1st Armored Division was approaching Tebaga Gap in Tunisia as night fell on March 25, causing the German and Italian infantry to withdraw from the Mareth Line. Earlier that day, the British Under-Secretary for Foreign Affairs, Richard Law, told the House of Commons of attempts by Bulgaria to de-Hellenize Western Thrace just as the Germans had tried to destroy Poland and Slovenia. Law, married to a woman from Rochester, New York, and later 1st Baron Coleraine, would write a sort of riposte to Thomas More in 1950, in a book arguing that the very idea of Utopia is evil, as it necessarily abolishes freedom and individual choice.

For the moment, his immediate concern was Greece, since that Feast of the Annunciation was also Greek Independence Day. The King of the Hellenes, George II, exiled in Cairo, sent a message of hope to his people, and shortly afterward it was announced that the Greek government would establish itself for the duration in the Middle East, save for a few departments remaining in London. The plan was to increase the number of guerrillas in Northern Greece by parachuting them in from Egypt, in preparation for an Allied invasion of the Balkans. As King Peter of Yugoslavia predicted that decisive battles would be fought in Europe in the next few months, the Greek Premier, Emmanuel Tsouderos, broadcast from Egypt to his homeland: "The trumpet call which shall announce the salvation of the enslaved peoples of Europe will sound, as I have every reason to believe, in the course of this year. All the omens show that our country is celebrating its national day in chains and bondage for the last time." Tsouderos had succeeded Alexandros Koryzis, who committed suicide in 1941 as the Germans marched on Athens. He would survive the war, serving his government in various capacities, dying in Genoa in 1956.

Quartered not far from Tsouderos in Cairo, the Very Rev. Arthur Hughes, Chargé d'Affaires of the Apostolic Delegation in Egypt, published a letter in a local newspaper, *La Bourse Egyptienne*:

"I have just received from Cardinal Maglione, Secretary of State to His Holiness, the assurance that the Holy See has worked and is still working for the protection of Jewish communities in the occupied countries, and that, despite the want of success of so many precious endeavours, the Holy Father does not cease to do everything that is possible. Only recently the Vatican has been strongly criticized by certain sections of the Central European Press for its defense of persecuted Jews, and for its articles in the *L'Osservatore Romano*."

19. A Flight from Reality

In mid-April, the Polish government in exile requested that the International Red Cross investigate the failure of the Soviet government to explain the fate of 8,300 Polish officers "taken prisoner" by the Red Army in the autumn of 1939. The Germans had just announced the discovery of mass graves in the Katyn Forest near Smolensk. Secretly, the Polish officers had been taken to Russia and executed by command of Lavrenti Beria, signed on March 5, 1940, under orders from Josef Stalin to eliminate "by shooting" the entire Polish Officers Corps. Added to the military victims were Polish civic leaders, physicians, professors, priests, and policemen – a total of 21,768, according to a report given to Nikita Khrushchev in 1959.

At the time of the April exhumations, the Soviets blamed the Nazis, and most of the West preferred to believe them. President Franklin Roosevelt dismissed the news from Katyn as "German propaganda and a German plot." The Soviet Union flamboyantly broke off diplomatic relations with the exiled Polish government for raising the subject. The final judgment came in November 2010, when the Russian State Duma acknowledged the massacre as the work of Stalin and the Soviet Politburo. When the mass graves were discovered in 1943, the archbishop of Krakow, Adam Sapieha, sent a priest by special train to Katyn to give a Christian burial to the murdered Poles. At this time, the same Archbishop Sapieha was providing secret instruction to seminarians – including Karol Wojtyła, who was also working as a boiler operator in the Solvay chemical plant. Some sort of resolution on the American side came in September 2012 when the U.S. National Archives released documents showing how

Churchill had informed Roosevelt that the British ambassador to the Polish government in exile, Owen O'Malley, was convinced that the Soviets were responsible for the massacre. The records also included a secret report of a special Congressional committee in 1952, concluding that Roosevelt had deliberately suppressed public knowledge of "one of the most barbarous international crimes in world history."

In another instance, the Soviets did correctly assign blame to the Germans for the massacres of Latvians – 80,000 in Riga and thousands more in Liepāja, Elava, and Władysław. But here the pot called the kettle black, for the Russians had orchestrated mass deportations of "anti-Soviet" elements in Latvia after the 1939 Molotov-Ribbentrop Pact.

Allied air raids against German U-boats intensified, and on April 18, in a ten-minute dogfight, the Allies lost just nine planes while downing 69 Luftwaffe planes en route to Tunisia. On the same day, the commander of the attack on Pearl Harbor, Adm. Isoroku Yamamoto, was shot down and killed by an American P-38 Lightning piloted by 1st Lt. Rex Barber over the Solomon Islands. The next day, Admiral Yamamoto's body, which had been thrown clear of the wreckage, was found in a jungle upright in his seat, still wearing white gloves and gripping the hilt of his ceremonial katana sword. His flight path had been discovered by breaking the Japanese flight code, and he had been targeted by order of President Roosevelt through Naval Secretary Frank Knox, to Admiral Chester Nimitz, and then to Admiral William Halsey. Roosevelt and Yamamoto had attended the same university in Cambridge, Massachusetts.

In more placid environs, neutral Ireland occupied itself with a debate over state control of schools. The School Attendance Bill would have required parents to send children only to government-approved schools. The Supreme Court found the bill unconstitutional. The Constitution of Eire acknowledged the right of parents to educate their children as they wish. The proposed legislation was taken as a step toward what the bishops warned would become a framework of the Servile State.

The full text of the Lenten Pastoral Letter of the Belgian bishops on slave workers reached England in mid-April, with its introductory protest against the confiscation of church bells by the Germans: "We solemnly declare that we will exert all our Episcopal authority to oppose a measure the sole object of which is to convert our bells into weapons of war and instruments of death." The seizure of the bells violated Articles 46, 52, and 56 of the Hague Convention, and to remain silent about the silencing of the bells "would be cowardly and treacherous." Then the bishops, led by Cardinal Van Roey, addressed the scandal of forced labor:

> "The requisitioning of human beings is utterly inexcusable; it is a violation of natural rights, of International Law, and of Christian ethics. . . . Moreover, the Christian faith teaches us that the Almighty, the Supreme Judge of conscience, sees everything, and that before His judgment-seat all human actions, without exception, will be judged according to the eternal laws."

According to the *Courier de Geneve*, a gathering of 7,000 French youth in Lille on March 21 had heard a fierce speech of Achille Cardinal Liénart decrying Nazi propaganda, which had twisted his words about the use of French workers in Germany:

> "I protest to you with all my strength against the use which was made of my words in the Press, because it was known that I could not publish any denial. . . . It was not my object to proclaim compulsory labour as a patriotic duty against the 'Bolshevik peril,' and I did not cite the example of Jeanne d'Arc in order 'to galvanize national sentiment against the English.' I also deny the right of the Press to interpret in its own manner the thoughts and intentions of the Holy Father."

The bishop of Le Puy, Msgr. Joseph-Marie-Eugene Martin, reiterated the cardinal's denunciation in the Basilica of St. Joseph at Le

Puy during a service of intercession for French prisoners of war. The German-controlled radio called the bishop a Gaullist cipher.

> "He may be entitled to his own opinion as a private person, but when he speaks from his pulpit he violates the precept that all the representatives of religion and all the congregations should support the Government of France. . . . Last Sunday [April 4] in his message to the nation, the Marshal [Pétain] himself answered the Bishop, in order to confound him and to incite him to be less frivolous."

Both Cardinal Liénart and Bishop Martin would live to attend the Second Vatican Council: Liénart, who had ordained Rev. Marcel Lefebvre to the priesthood in 1929 and episcopate in 1947, would be a prominent liberal voice at the council, while Martin would caution against the risk of schism if a vernacular liturgy were permitted.

On April 19, more than 2,000 S.S. men under General Jürgen Stroop, acting under a directive of Heinrich Himmler to disperse the Warsaw ghetto, were amazed to find themselves resisted and actually repulsed by the Jews, who were lightly armed. Four days later, personal orders came from Hitler to use "utmost severity." On that same Feast of St. George, patron of soldiers, British Lt. Gen. Frederick Morgan assumed command of a headquarters in London for planning what would become the Normandy invasion.

Simultaneously, the Swedish *Svenska Dagbladet* printed a letter from the archbishop of Zagreb, Msgr. Aloysius Stepinac, to the Italian ambassador to the Croatian puppet state. The Italians had been exploiting conflicts between Croats and Serbs to make them seem ideological rather than ethnic: "I must protest energetically against the incredible atrocities committed by Italian troops against the defenceless populations in the districts of Krasic, Vidovina and Brovac, where several villages have been burnt down. . . . Even if some Communists should have succeeded in taking refuge there, I can vouch that there were not, and are not now, any Communists among the village population."

After the war, Archbishop Stepinac would be a victim of the new Communist government, imprisoned after a show trial. Pope Pius XII created him a cardinal in 1952, and he died in 1960, having most certainly been poisoned by Communist agents. A Mass was offered for him in Rome by Pope John XXIII, with whom he had collaborated in wartime to save Croatian Jews. On October 3, 1998, outside Zagreb in Marija Bistrica, half a million Croats watched Pope John Paul II beatify him as a martyr.

In the grim April days, Vatican Radio announced that the German government had shut down the few remaining Catholic diocesan journals (*kirchliche Bistumblatter*). Adolf Cardinal Bertram, archbishop of Breslau and dean of the German Catholic hierarchy, had long been outspoken in the pulpit and press against the Nazis. In 1940 he had called their *Lebensborn* eugenics program a form of "institutionalized adultery." Without any print media, Cardinal Bertram urged the people to pay ever closer attention to what was preached in sermons. And many did, for a Stockholm correspondent reported to the Brooklyn *Tablet* that an issue of Goebbels' *Die Weltliteratur* a few months past was increasingly perplexed by "the flight of the German masses from reality." The complaint was against the "interior emigration" from National Socialism caused by "the superstition of religion, which is taking hold among all classes, both educated and uneducated. The influence of religion on the life of the German people is becoming extraordinary. It is a growing danger for Nazism." The article pointed out a lecturer in the University of Leipzig, Ernst Wiechert, who had once been a staunch Nazi, but lately "almost openly contradicted" it. Worse was a writer who had just published a book with a religious theme: "It is incredible! . . . A German dares to praise the Old Testament!"

Sisley Huddleston was rather more obtuse in his own flight from reality. The English journalist and ardent Francophile had lived a long while in Paris after World War I, writing for both the *Times* back in London and the *Christian Science Monitor*. In April

1943, he became a French citizen, spent time interviewing Pétain, and chose Good Friday to broadcast on Vichy radio that he had done so in the interest of European unity. All European virtue came from the Greek and Romans (mostly the Greeks), and the Bolsheviks were about to destroy all that. From London, the *Tablet* astringently commented: "But he had no word to say about Germany, wherein the Mediterranean winds blew late and incompletely, and whence through Hegel and Feuerbach and Marx the ideology of Soviet Russia came."

Huddleston was an impatient and unrepresentative disciple of the brilliant pioneer of pan-Europeanism, the Austro-Hungarian Count Richard Nikolaus von Coudenhove-Kalergi who, in 1943, was a professor at New York University. The character Victor Laszlo in the film *Casablanca* was based on him. The Count, whom Hitler loathed as "everybody's bastard," had been admired by Archduke Otto von Habsburg, Aristide Briand, Albert Einstein, Horace Mann, Sigmund Freud, and later by Winston Churchill and Charles de Gaulle; he was an anti-Nazi and foe of anti-Semitism (like his Catholic father, who annually walked out of Good Friday services at the mention of the "perfidious Jews"). For all his pan-Europeanism, Coudenhove-Kalergi's mother was Japanese. In comparison with him, Huddleston's intellect was decidedly derivative and apathetic to historical facts. In 1944, he was arrested by the Free French as a collaborator and went on to write books about the horrors of the liberation of France, the patriotism of Pétain, and the virginity of Queen Elizabeth.

In a letter of April 30 to Bishop von Preysing, Pius XII described with unusual candor the theory of nuance he had deliberately equated with prudence in his public statements: "We give to the pastors who are working on the local level the duty of determining if and to what degree the danger of reprisals and of various forms of oppression occasioned by episcopal declarations . . . *ad maiora mala vitanda* (to avoid worse) . . . seem to advise caution. Here lies one of the reasons, why We impose self-restraint on Ourselves in our speeches; the experience, that we made in 1942 with papal addresses, which We authorized to be forwarded to the Believers, justifies our opinion, as far as We see . . . The Holy See has done whatever was in its power, with charitable, financial and moral assistance. To say nothing of the substantial sums which we spent in American money for the fares of immigrants."

In England, the slogans still were of the "Keep Calm and Carry On" sort. In a discussion of Easter eggs during the food shortage, one correspondent commented that the crocodile's egg, when boiled, tastes almost like that of the domestic hen, though he neglected to explain where crocodiles were to be found in Sussex. As for meat rationing, it was remembered that the Roman statesman and aesthete Mycaenas cooked donkeys, and the Roman emperor Heliogabalus (218–222) served his dinner guests camels' feet, but "he degraded the imperial office to the lowest point by most shameful vices, which had their origin in certain rites of oriental naturalistic religion." On a more sober note, word came from Cambridge University that, due to the shortage of proper material, mortarboards would be optional dress for the duration.

20. The Soul Means Nothing

Benedetto Croce died in 1952, the same year in which Albert Einstein had to protest to his friend Maurice Solovine, "lest you think that weakened by age I have fallen into the hands of priests." In 1943, Croce had to do something similar, as his essays on philosophic idealism increasingly gave the impression that he would be a Christian: "The truth is that although the whole of past history converges upon us, and we are the children of history as a whole, the ethics and religion of antiquity were vanquished and resolved in the Christian idea of conscience and moral inspiration, and in the new idea of God in Whom we live and move and have our being, and Who cannot be either Zeus or Jahwe, nor even (in the spirit of the adulation of which he has in our day been made the object) the Germanic Woden; and specifically, therefore, in our moral life and thought, we felt ourselves to be the direct descendants of Christianity."

The tumult of the war seemed to vindicate his concept of history, nurtured by Vico, as "philosophy in motion," and he was certain that National Socialism was bad philosophy. In his idealism and pronounced opposition to Fascism, Christianity was an effort at expressing truth, rather than truth itself, but it was increasingly being vindicated as a sublime contradiction of lies against truth, as time avenges the propagation of deceit:

> "It is easy to see that, in our present age, we are by no means outside the limits set by Christianity, and that we, like the first Christians, are still struggling to reconcile the ever renewed, sharp and terrible contrasts between immanence and transcendence, between the

morality of the conscience and that of precept and the laws, between ethicism and utilitarianism, between liberty and authority, between the earthly and the heavenly denseness which exist in man, and success in reconciling them in one or other of their individual forms fills us with joy and internal tranquility. . . ."

Croce was constantly hounded by Benito Mussolini, his library ransacked, and in 1944 he would flee Sorrento for Capri to thwart a Fascist attempt to kidnap him and deposit him in a German U-boat. As Croce was ruminating, the British First Army captured Tunis and the Americans seized Bizerte. More than 250,000 Axis soldiers were captured in North Africa on May 13 when the German Afrika Korps and Italian troops surrendered, the Allies having lost about three thousand men in the Tunis area. The scale of victory was redolent of Agincourt, and the Allies did not fail to take heart from it. On May 19, the Allies bombed Sardinia and Sicily as prelude to the invasion of Italy. Bloodier was the Japanese massacre of 30,000 Chinese civilians and rape of thousands of women in Changjiao, Hunan, on May 11.

In the United States, Winston Churchill was meeting with Franklin D. Roosevelt, preparing for the invasion of France. Five states – Michigan, Wisconsin, Connecticut, Massachusetts, and New York – were crucial in the calculus of the next year's presidential election, with Catholics considered the swing votes. A Gallup poll showed that less than half of the Americans thought Russia could be trusted when the war ended. This was despite the pro-Stalin propaganda efforts of Joseph E. Davies, former U.S. ambassador to the Soviet Union. At the behest of Roosevelt, his Soviet-friendly book *Mission to Moscow* was made into a Warner Brothers film, with Walter Huston as Davies and Ann Harding as Mrs. Davies, the heiress Marjorie Merriweather Post. When he was ambassador, Davies had whitewashed Stalin's show trials and told his wife that the gunshots that could be heard at night in Moscow as political prisoners were being killed were just workers using construction drills. Even the film's own producer, Robert Buckner, admitted, "I did not fully respect Mr. Davies' integrity, both before, during and after the film. I knew that FDR had brainwashed him." Davies met with Roosevelt four times between July 1942 and March 1943 to discuss the script. The final screen version portrays an avuncular, pipe-smoking Stalin who annexed Finland in 1940 as an act of altruism to protect that land from the Nazis. The Moscow purge trials of 1937 were models of jurisprudence and Trotsky was a Nazi agent. Davies himself introduced the film in a pompous prologue: "I felt it was my duty to tell the truth." The crudeness of its propaganda notwithstanding, the film was well-received in *The New York Times* on April 30, 1943, by its critic Bosley Crowther for portraying Russia as "a true and most reliable ally." With an advisory that it had "no hesitancy in stepping on a few tender toes," Crowther went on to say that "Mission to Moscow" conveyed "a realistic impression of fact" and was "a valuable influence to more clear-eyed and searching thought." Perhaps because he was stung by responses to his review, including a scathing one by John Dewey, Crowther qualified his remarks on May 9 by saying that the film should have shown "a little less ecstasy."

Charles Bohlin, future ambassador to the Soviet Union (1953–1957) was fluent in Russian, unlike Davies, on whose staff in Moscow he had served. Bohlin later wrote of Davies: "I can only guess at the motivation for his reporting. He ardently desired to make a success of a pro-Soviet line and was probably reflecting the views of some of Roosevelt's advisers to enhance his political standing at home." In May 1943, as the film was appearing in American theaters, Roosevelt sent Davies back to Moscow to arrange a private meeting with Stalin in Fairbanks, Alaska, which never came to pass. Chip Bohlin became Roosevelt's interpreter at Teheran and Yalta.

In May, the new bishop of Hertogenbosch (Bois le Duc) in southern Holland, Msgr. Willem Pieter Mutsaers, appointed Msgr. F. N. J. Henriks as his vicar general. It was a symbolic act, since Bishop Henriks had been sent to a German concentration camp in 1942 and had not been heard from since. Holland was placed under martial law, as the Germans feared an Allied landing. Deportations to Germany of Dutch reservists and N.C.O.s, begun in 1942, increased to about half a million men, affecting nearly every family in Holland. Students in the Dutch universities attempted protests against Nazi revision of their academic syllabus, as did students at the Sorbonne and the Paris Grandes Écoles, who sent a public letter directly to Marshal Philippe Pétain:

> "For more than two years, forgetting their rowdy traditions, the students of the University of Paris have abstained from demonstrations. But our silence has never implied an acceptance of events of which we were the distressed spectators. Above all, the brutal deportation of thousands of French workers has provoked our indignation."

A French priest wrote to the Catholic press in the United States about living conditions among the clergy. The Bishop of Tulle, Msgr. Aimable Chassaigne, had been forced to reduce the living wage of his priests to 4,000 francs, which was barely survival level. The bishop of Mende, Msgr. Francois-Louis Auvity, appealed to the populace to give potatoes, beans, and chestnuts to the clergy. He closed his seminary and sent the students home because he could no longer feed them.

The apostolic administrator of Estonia, the Most Reverend Eduard Profittlich, S.J., was found alive in a prison camp in the Urals, not having been heard of since the Russians arrested him in 1941. With the increasing prospect of invasion, penitential processions began in Italy, starting with one on Good Friday in Milan from the cathedral to the shrine of the Madonna of San Celso. The procession was led by the great crucifix with which St. Charles Borromeo had led similar processions to ward off famine, pestilence, and war. In Bologna, the body of St. Dominic was removed to a specially constructed bomb-proof chapel. In Turin, the Holy Shroud was taken from the chapel in the royal palace to a secret location known only to its three guardians: the king, Prince Umberto, and the cardinal archbishop.

On May 5, the Secretary of State for the Holy See again wrote to the Slovakian Legation condemning "the forcible removal of persons belonging to the Jewish race . . . The Holy See would fail in its Divine mandate if it did not deplore these measures, which gravely damage man in his natural right, merely for the reason that these people belong to a certain race." On the same day, the secretariat prepared a memorandum:

> "The Jews. A dreadful situation. There were approximately four and a half million of them in Poland before the war; today the estimate is that not even a hundred thousand remain there, including those who have come from other countries under German occupation. . . . There are special death camps near Lublin and Brest-Litovsk. It is said that by the hundreds they are shut up in chambers where they are gassed to death and then transported in tightly sealed cattle trucks with lime on their floors."

A few days later in Bulgaria, the secretary of the Jewish Agency for Palestine personally asked Archbishop Roncalli, the future Pope John XXIII, "to thank the Holy See for the happy outcome of the steps taken on behalf of the Israelites in Slovakia."

Vatican Radio was broadcasting to Russia, but not with much success. A Russian listener described his Orwellian world:

> "All private sets in Russia were confiscated at the outbreak of the war, and were replaced by loudspeakers fed from reception sets in so-called 'radio junctions' in factories, Army units, collective farm offices and other Government-controlled institutions. Thus the only potential and not very reliable listeners whom non-Soviet stations broadcasting in Russian may hope to address are the State-employed radio operators, who, in their spare time (and with their sets carefully

disconnected from the loudspeakers), may indulge in the universal pastime of 'twiddling the knobs.' These will be mostly young people, the great majority of them grown up since the Revolution, and therefore without even the most elementary religious education. The three first Vatican broadcasts in Russian have used a far too involved theological terminology to be comprehensible to people who, as regards religions, could be approached only in the language used by missionaries bringing the Cross to a race of a comparatively low standard of civilization."

The bishop of Annecy, Msgr. Auguste-Leon-Alexis Cesbron, wrote an Easter pastoral letter that was translated and circulated among English-speaking Catholics at the beginning of May. Its conclusion challenged the budding season of spring:

"But the trouble of these times, with the prolonged privations, the insecurity which is so painful to us, the nervousness created by our misfortunes, the anguish which we felt about our future, known or unknown – all these form an inextricable confusion, in which is hidden secretly manoeuvering and scarcely perceptible, the often mortal enemies of the souls of our youth. You hear it said that it is intended to form a strong and healthy youth, and through it to rediscover the soul of France. But what one too often sees leads one to believe that, for many people, the soul means nothing."

In 1950, the same bishop would consecrate a new church in the French Alps parish of Assy. It was a showpiece of modern ecclesiastical art, with windows by Rouault, tapestries by Lurcat, a Leger mosaic, and drawings by Matisse. Bishop Cesbron kept his thoughts to himself about the success of it all, but he ordered the removal of a large green bronze crucifix by Germain Richter. It had no cross. The corpus had no discernible features. Richter explained that "the cross has been taken with the suffering into the flesh, and its outlines can just be made out coming from the undersides of the arms. There is no face because God is the spirit, and faceless." A Paris journal protested its removal and called its critics "partisans of mediocrity." A local woodcutter, a survivor of the war, sided with his bishop and said that the faceless figure was "evil."

21. A Time for Spies

May was flush with the most colorfully camouflaged spy networks in every government, and the Allied bombing of Sicily and Sardinia on May 19 and 20, as prelude to the invasion of Italy, punctuated one of the most celebrated espionage tricks of the war: Operation Mincemeat. As the brainchild of Admiral John Godfrey, director of British naval intelligence, it arranged for a corpse dressed as an airman and laden with bogus documents to be washed ashore in Spain. The corpse wore religious medals, as it was thought that a Catholic might be buried more quickly by the Spanish, thus avoiding a lengthy autopsy. There followed an almost comic contest between Spanish naval officials and the German Abwehr in Madrid, teased along by the British consul. Intelligence agents working from London included Ewen Montagu, a barrister and son of the immensely wealthy Jewish peer Lord Louis Montagu and a benignly eccentric Oxford geographer; Charles Cholmondeley; and Commander Ian Fleming, codename 17F. After the war, Admiral Godfrey devoted himself to charities and founded the Chelsea Centre for Spastic Children, while muttering that Fleming had used him as the model for James Bond's "unsavoury" superior "M" in the novels.

Copies of the forged documents eventually came to the desk of Hitler himself, whose skepticism was conquered by assurances of their authenticity by his intelligence advisor, Baron Alexis von Roenne. The aristocratic wounded war hero of the First World War was a devout Catholic, appalled at the invasion of Poland, and was in fact a counterspy by his own devices. The German decision a year later to expect an Allied invasion at

Calais was also based on von Roenne's disinformation. As a friend of the conspirator Claus von Stauffenberg, von Roenne was one of those left to die slowly on meat hooks in Berlin's Plötzensee prison in 1944, all filmed for the Führer's viewing delectation. His last letter to his wife read: "In a moment now I shall be going home to our Lord in complete calm and in the certainty of salvation."

There was muffled jubilation in the war intelligence rooms of London when intercepted dispatches showed that the hoax had succeeded: The Germans had decided that the Allies indeed were aiming for Sardinia and Greece in the Peloponnese rather than Sicily. Churchill, still in Washington on the code-named "Trident" conference, enjoyed the deception. Mussolini was suspicious, and so was Goebbels, but Hitler was persuaded and the Duce changed his own mind by May 20. He stepped up anti-Anglo Saxon propaganda, accusing the Allies of hiding anti-personnel devices in children's chocolates and women's cosmetics.

Having been made commander in chief of the German navy the previous January, Admiral Karl Donitz began a recall of U-boats in the Atlantic on May 24 because of heavy losses, his own son having died on one five days earlier. He too had been persuaded by Operation Mincemeat. Hitler trusted him and would in fact designate him his heir just before shooting himself. The foreign minister, Joachim von Ribbentrop, was certain that the Allies intended to invade the Balkans by way of Greece, having been told so by Ernst Kaltenbrunner, chief of the *Reichssicherheitshauptamt*, the main security office cobbled together by Himmler when he combined the Security Service and the Gestapo.

Lord Robert Vansittart – the retired former chief diplomat advisor to the British government, though a member of the Privy Council since 1940 – had been Churchillian in his opposition to appeasement. His memoirs, *Lessons of My Life*, were being read widely in May. While respecting the anti-Nazism of Michael Cardinal von Faulhaber, he was of the opinion that Faulhaber's predecessor, Franziskus Cardinal von Bettinger, had favored unrestricted submarine warfare, setting a precedent for the Nazis. One reviewer pointed out that the case was the opposite: The cardinal had persuaded the king of Bavaria to join the Emperor (and future Blessed) Karl of Austria and Pope Benedict XV in a protest to the Kaiser against such use of submarines. In the 1920s, Cardinal Faulhaber belonged to the International Catholic League against Anti-Semitism and Racism (*Amici Israel*) and helped write the German text of Pius XI's encyclical *Mit Brennender Sorge*, with its prescient warning about Nazi racial theories. In 1938, on Kristalnacht, Cardinal Faulhaber had lent a truck to the chief rabbi of Munich to help salvage objects from his synagogue. When the war was over, on a pleasant June day in 1951, in the cathedral of Freising, Cardinal Faulhaber ordained Joseph Ratzinger to the priesthood, his last ordination before his death the following June.

"*Republicae Christianae hostium orientali internece et clade Africana laetam in spem. . .*" was some of the ornate Latinity inscribed on the paschal candle in the cathedral of Malines, Belgium, rejoicing that, in the 1,943rd year of the Incarnation, in the reign of Pope Pius XII and the episcopate of Jozef-Ernest Cardinal van Roey, and in the reign of Leopold III, the Nazi and Communist enemies of Christianity were destroying each other in the East, and the African campaign was a sign of hope. Cardinal van Roey had revived an old custom of recording on the Easter candle the recent blessings of God. By May the Nazi papers quivered with rage, and in Ghent the *Vooruit* accused the cardinal of making common cause with Freemasonry and rejoicing in the "African disaster" and the death of troops along the Eastern front. "We will not tolerate this any longer. We are sick of the political wailings of the Cardinal and his clergy."

Simultaneously, the Office of War Information in Washington published a summary of the petition from the German Catholic bishop to the Reich minister for Church affairs, the education minister, and the Church of the Reich chancellery, sent just before Christmas. In the name of all the German bishops, Adolf Cardinal Bertram, Archbishop of Breslau, protested against "measures of officials of the [Nazi] party and Government that are directed against the Church and against Christianity" and "violations of the free practice of the religion of Catholic Christians in the territories that recently have come to Germany." These territories included Alsace-Lorraine, Luxembourg, Poland, and Yugoslavia. The bishops listed the expulsion of priests to concentration camps, dissolution of church organizations, confiscation of property, and the closing of monasteries. There was no official response, but Nazi authorities at Baden announced that the property of the St. Vincent de Paul Society "is to be confiscated, as the activities of this association are hostile to the people and the State."

In reaction to the formation of the compulsory National Socialist medical organization, "The Physicians' Chamber," 97 percent of the doctors in the Netherlands refused to join, according to the *Svenska Dagbladet*. The Nazis had tried to force enrollment by deducting a membership fee from the salaries paid by the State. The physicians went on strike, even removing the brass name plates from their offices. Soon the government capitulated. The two principal centers of Catholic education in Holland, Nijmegen University and Tilburg Commercial High School, were closed when students refused to sign a "declaration of loyalty" to the German Reich and military.

The Vatican Radio on May 12 broadcast a message to German listeners telling of the forced registration of Jews in Croatia and the subsequent protest in Zagreb by Archbishop Aloysius Stepinac against Dr. Ante Pavelić who was the *Poglavnik*, or head, of the Croatian puppet state and of the Fascist party, the Ustaše. The following Sunday, the archbishop preached: "No worldly power, no political organization, has the right to persecute a man on account of the race to which he belongs. Christian bishops oppose this, and will fight against such persecutions." A speech he gave on October 24, 1942, is typical of many that he made refuting Nazi theory: "All men and all races are children of God; all without distinction. Those who are Gypsies, black, European, or Aryan all have the same rights. . . .

For this reason, the Catholic Church had always condemned, and continues to condemn, all injustice and all violence committed in the name of theories of class, race, or nationality. It is not permissible to persecute Gypsies or Jews because they are thought to be an inferior race."

The Associated Press reported that "by 1942 Stepinac had become a harsh critic" of the Nazi puppet regime, condemning its "genocidal policies, which killed tens of thousands of Serbs, Jews, Gypsies, and Croats." The Vatican maintained its nunciature in Belgrade, recognizing the legitimacy of the royal government in exile. Pavelić was believed to have plotted the assassination of King Alexander of Yugoslavia in Marseilles on a state visit to France in 1934. The king had urged the appointment of Stepinac as Archbishop of Zagreb to counter the nationalist Archbishop Ivan Saric of Sarajevo. When Pavelić came to power, Saric embraced the Ustaše policies, and even penned an ode to Pavelić:

For God himself was at thy side, thou good and strong one,
So that thou mightest perform thy deeds for the Homeland . . .
And against the Jews, who had all the money.

Pavelić's Ustaše regime, known to be butchers even in the estimation of the Nazis, was not, contrary to some later revisionists, recognized diplomatically by the Holy See. Pius XII received Pavelić in audience once, or possibly twice, only on the condition that he attend as a private citizen without entourage or any publicity. After the war, Saric escaped a war crime trial by fleeing to Austria and then to Spain where he wrote a book to justify himself, praising Pius XII.

Within a week of the May 12 broadcast, the official order for Jewish registration was rescinded, but it is estimated that during the course of the war, Croatia had the highest rate of genocide in proportion to population of any European country: more than 200,000 Serbs, nearly 30,000 Jews, 26,000 Gypsies – including elderly men, women, and children – many hacked to death or burned alive. The Ustaše action was excessive even compared to the Nazi bestiary, and German General Edmund von Glaise-Horstenau wrote in a dispatch that they had "gone mad." After the war, using forged credentials, Pavelić was hidden by Jesuits in a monastery near Naples and fled to Argentina in 1948. Under a pseudonym, he became a security advisor to Juan Peron. In 1957 he was shot – the work of Yugoslavian intelligence – but he survived and was granted exile in Spain, where he died in 1959.

The Court Circular announced in London on May 14 that Francis D'Arcy Godolphin Osborne, as British minister to the Holy See, had been received by King George VI who conferred upon him a knighthood, the insignia of Knight Commander of St. Michael and St. George. Recently found correspondence documents that on November 7, 1944, Osborne had notified Franklin C. Gowen, an assistant to his U.S. counterpart at the Holy See, Myron Taylor, that the Pope should be dissuaded from making what D'Arcy feared would be a radio appeal on behalf of the Jews in Hungary. It would have "very serious political repercussions," as it would anger the Russians.

On May 16, Archbishop Francis Spellman arrived in Istanbul from Beirut, continuing his mysterious travels ostensibly to visit U.S. troops. This detour, he told the Turkish Press, was to visit his "old friend" the Archbishop of Mesembria, Msgr. Angelo Roncalli, who had been Apostolic Delegate to Turkey since 1934. When Roncalli eventually became Pope, it was said that Spellman was decidedly unhappy with the election of his "old friend." The New York prelate was received by the Turkish president in Ankara on May 18 and then returned to Syria, and from there he set off for India and China on unspecified business.

The day before his arrival in Istanbul, nine students at Downside, the Benedictine school in Somerset, were killed when an RAF airplane crashed on the cricket field. The monks of the abbey sang the Office of the Dead when the bodies of the boys were brought into the choir on the 18th; the abbot, the Rt. Rev. R. S. Trafford, sang the Pontifical Requiem Mass on the 19th. Sixty officers and men of the Fleet Air Arm provided a guard of honor as the bodies were buried in a common grave in the monks' cemetery. Messages of sympathy were received from the apostolic delegate, Queen Mary, and the lords of the admiralty.

An obituary of Flying-Officer Charles Robert Cecil Augustus Allberry, killed in action at the age of 32 in Nederweert, Holland, spoke of one who was "daring and merry as well as kind." The vice-master of Christ's College, Cambridge, wrote in the *Times* that he had already attained, at the age of 27, front rank as a Coptic scholar by his edition of a Manichaean psalter, which led to his appointment as editor of the *Journal of Egyptian Archeology*. His Coptic dictionary was unfinished at his death. His friend C. P. Snow based a character on him in his novel *The Light and the Dark*. Allberry had been received into the Catholic Church in May 1941.

22. The Health and Happiness of Baby

In the Teutonic gloom spreading from Tunisia to Stalingrad, the Luftwaffe engineered a glimmer of fresh resiliency with the inaugural test flight of a Messerschmitt Me 262 jet reaching 520 mph on May 22. In those same hours, Stalin was dissolving the Third International, or Comintern, on the first anniversary of the formal Soviet alliance with Britain. The propaganda effort to abate western fears of Soviet plans for world conquest garnered the signature of the French communists André Marty and Marcel Thorez and the Spanish "La Pasionaria" Isidora Ibárruri Gomez. Whether the Nationalist rumors were true that she had killed a priest by biting his throat with her teeth in the Civil War, her son did indeed die fighting at Stalingrad. The modesty of Marxist intentions was quickly forgotten after 1945. The opportunism recalled the final dissolution of the First International in 1876 in Philadelphia, to Marx's dismay, after its rupture at the Hague Congress of 1872, in response to world chagrin at the Paris Commune. The day after Stalin's public gesture, 800 Allied planes launched the fiercest air raid of the war so far, dropping 2,000 tons of bombs in an attack on Dortmünd in Germany, killing 700 civilians.

Due to the special circumstances of occupied Poland, Pope Pius XII appointed Archbishop Godfrey, Apostolic Delegate to Great Britain, to be Chargé d'Affaires accredited to the Polish Government. During the First World War, the appointment of the future Pope Pius XI, Achille Ratti, as Apostolic Visitator of the Holy See and then as Apostolic Nuncio was understood as a sign of Pope Benedict XV's confidence in Poland's future. In 1939, the new Nuncio, Msgr. Philippo Cortesi, went into exile in

Rumania and Hungary with the Polish Government, doing welfare work among the Polish troops until health forced him to return to Italy. On this year's Polish National Day, May 3, Pope Pius XII had Cortesi deliver a message to Dr. Kazimierz Papee, the Polish ambassador to the Holy See and informal representative of the Polish government in exile, saying that the day of Poland's delivery was approaching. The Pope told Polish pilgrims: "I profoundly deplore the sufferings of the Polish nation. I give it my blessing, and I wish that Poland may be larger, stronger, and even more Catholic after this war." Papee formally thanked the Pope for his assistance to prisoners of war, internees, and refugees and gave him a painting of our Lady of Czestochowa. The Pope's meeting with Papee on May 21 was taken as a de facto recognition of the exiled Polish government. This somewhat assuaged the feelings of the president of the Polish government in exile, Wladyslaw Raczkiewicz, who ruefully interpreted the January appointment of Msgr. Hilarius Bretinger as apostolic administrator for the Wartheland as the Holy See's recognition, albeit unexpressed, of the fragmentation of Poland. According to his memoirs published in 1954, Papee expressed to Luigi Cardinal Maglione, the Papal Secretary of State, some exasperation at the Pope's hesitancy to speak in other than diplomatic language about the situation in Poland, rather in the same way Bishop Karol Radonski had complained in writing directly to the Pope during his exile in London. In one audience, according to Papee, the Pope addressed Papee: "I have listened again and again to your representations about our unhappy children in Poland. Must I be given the same story yet again?" Pope John XXIII had him replaced in 1958, but he remained in Rome after his diplomatic credentials were withdrawn, dying there in 1979.

Nazi efforts to refashion marriage as a celebration of its mythology were spreading. The Flemish *De SS Man* described a state ritual that had been cobbled together, rather like the Deist cults of the French Revolution: "Untersturmführer Van Dijck admitted the bride into the Sibbe community in the name of the

SS-Reichführer. The ceremony ended with the SS Treueleid and a threefold Sieg Heil for the only Germanic Führer. Some old Germanic traditions were observed at dinner, which lent deep meaning to the whole ceremony."

On May 18th, Dr. Friedrich, chief German spokesman on Radio Paris, was disappointed that so many Catholics continued to fear National-Socialism. The blame belonged to the Vatican: "A careful perusal of the Papal Press, the reports on interviews of high ecclesiastical authorities with Pius XI, and the study of the Encyclicals, have enabled me now clearly to realize the crushing responsibility of the Church in unleashing the present war. Just as the Vatican had condemned Fascism, so it had, inevitably, to condemn National-Socialism. Was it not a fact that these two revolutions were going to attempt to restore to all men the consciousness of their own dignity, and thus to come into conflict with the Church in the spiritual sphere? As soon as the Führer assumed power, in 1933, the Vatican let loose its hostility." Friedrich recalled how the Pope had made Cardinal Innitzer stop giving the "Heil Hitler" salute and had said that anti-Semitism was incompatible with Christianity and had approved Cardinal Mundelein's defamation of Hitler. "National-Socialism tried to settle all conflicts with the Church; the Church rejected the hand offered to her. May she bear the responsibility for this in the annals of history."

Gracing the cover of *Time* magazine for May 24 was the newly appointed First Sea Lord, Andrew Browne Cunningham, later 1st Viscount of Hyndhope. In 1943 he had directed the naval supply operations in the Western Mediterranean littoral. In that issue, some readers wrote to the editor about John L. Lewis's breaking of a pledge not to strike during the war. Half a million United Mine Workers had stopped work at his direction. An Army aerial gunner, Staff Sergeant F. M. Hilary of Orlando, Florida let loose "The men who fly over Europe through a blanket of flak would be greatly amazed if they returned to the U.S. and found that it had been forced into totalitarianism as a last resort against men of the Lewis ilk." Essa Gladney of Tahlequah,

Oklahoma said succinctly: "My honest opinion is that as a public service and a part of the war effort, somebody should shoot John L. Lewis." Three Army privates, John Boulet, Clinton Draper and Stanley Urba, proposed: "Sirs: We the undersigned request that you use your influence to obtain John L. Lewis for our bayonet practice."

Among other events of May 24, the eldest daughter of the Duke of Marlborough, and great-granddaughter of William K. Vanderbilt, married a U.S. Naval Lieutenant from New Jersey. The 48-year-old violinist Albert Stroessel died of a heart attack in Manhattan, and so also died, 39 years older, William Andrew Johnson, who had been named for his slave owner, President Andrew Johnson, and had been given a silver-headed walking stick by President Roosevelt in 1937.

On that same day, a 32-year-old physician arrived in the concentration camp of Auschwitz-Birkenau to assist the chief garrison physician, SS-Standortarzt Eduard Wirths. Josef Mengele had a Ph.D. in Physical Anthropology from the University of Munich and two years later, in 1937, he had been awarded another Ph.D, from the University of Frankfurt's Institute for Hereditary Biology and Racial Hygiene (Rassenhygiene) under the direction of Dr. Ernst Rudin. Mengele attended many of Rudin's lectures and admired him, as did the American eugenicist Margaret Sanger, publisher of some of Rudin's papers in the United States. Mengele had a particular fascination with the phenomenon of "heterochromia," or different colored eyes in the same person. Standing on the railroad platform at Auschwitz, he looked for twins and used them for his more modest experiments. More ghoulish were his surgeries without anesthesia, live autopsies, and vivisections on pregnant women. This "Todesengel," or Angel of Death, as he was called by his victims, compelled two Jews to assist him, a pediatrician Berthold Epstein, whose own family was exterminated in the camp, and Miklos Nyiszli, an Hungarian pathologist. They were able to testify against Mengele later, although he slipped through American custody and fled to Buenos Aires where he became an illegal, but much experienced, abortionist. Arraigned for the death of one his "patients," he was released by the judge and eventually worked his way via Paraguay to Brazil where he died an utterly banal death, evidently by drowning in the surf, in 1979. He never understood why he had been criticized for his medical science, and was disgusted when Albrecht Speer apologized for deeds of the Reich.

Contraception and abortion had been earnest policies of the Reich, to subdue non-Aryan populations, thus exempting Norwegians, Danes, Dutch, and Flemish Belgians. Three weeks before Mengele arrived at Auschwitz, Professor Erhard Wetzel, Racial Administrator for the Reich's Eastern Territories Ministry, issued a memorandum:

> "Every propaganda means, especially the press, radio, and movies, as well as pamphlets, booklets, and lectures, must be used to instill in the Russian population the idea that it is harmful to have several children. We must emphasize the expenses that children cause, the good things that people could have had with the money spent on them. We could also hint at the dangerous effect of child-bearing on a woman's health. Paralleling such propaganda, a large-scale campaign would be launched in favor of contraceptive devices. A contraceptive industry must be established. Neither the circulation and sale of contraceptives nor abortions must be prosecuted. It will even be necessary to open special institutions for abortion, and to train midwives and nurses for this purpose."

Zyklon-B gas used in the death camps was manufactured by I G Farben (Interessen-Gemeinschaft Farbenindustrie AG). After the war trials of its officers, the company was broken up into units including Hoechst AG. Today it is a wholly owned subsidiary of Sanofi-Aventis. In 1997, Hoechst AG bought the French pharmaceutical company Roussel Uclaf S.A. which had developed the RU-486 abortion pill now on the commercial market.

As Mengele was experimenting on babies, or destroying them altogether, the British government was issuing guidelines for infant nutrition: "Right from the start is the time to plan the health and happiness of Baby and yourself...The old saying 'lose a tooth for every child' need not be true for you if you eat rightly. And the right foods now, help you quickly to recover your strength and energy after Baby is born." The Crown allowed expectant mothers seven pints of milk a week, three eggs, orange juice and cod liver oil. "Get a medical certificate from your doctor, certified midwife or health visitor. Hand or send this with your ration book to your Food Office. . . There is little risk of too much meat nowadays, but your doctor will tell you whether to cut it down during the last months."

23. Different Kinds of Diplomats

As Foreign Minister, and Viceroy of India before that, Lord Edward Halifax was the preferred choice of the Conservative Party and the King to succeed Chamberlain as Prime Minister, but he knew he was no match for Churchill and did not press his case. In this he showed an altruism which was commonly admired, notwithstanding his naïveté as an appeaser in the years building up to the war. His father, the 2nd Viscount Halifax, had been a leading Anglo-Catholic layman, famous for his ecumenical conversations with Cardinal Mercier of Belgium. He embraced his father's ardent piety, along with a stamina that made him a fox-hunter and shooter to be reckoned with despite a withered arm and missing hand. A few months into office, Churchill had him appointed ambassador to Washington, and quickly upstaged him by his personal diplomacy with Roosevelt. Lord and Lady Halifax spent themselves on morale-boosting tours of the United States and Canada after their middle son was killed in action.

He was Chancellor of Oxford and remained so until his death in 1959. The University of Laval in Quebec conferred an honorary degree on the Viscount (later the 1st Earl of Halifax) on May 29, 1943. The acceptance speech, broadcast on the Canadian Broadcasting Corporation, hymned what he had inherited from the High Church ideals of the Oxford Movement. "There has never yet been a movement to destroy Christianity, which, sooner or later, has not found itself obliged to face the necessity of trying to find something to replace it. . . . wherever we find a false idea about men, its origin lies in a false idea of God." He quoted the 1942 Christmas pastoral letter of the bishop of Berlin, Konrad von Preysing Lichtenegg-Moss: "The moment mankind – whether as individuals, as larger communities, or as nations – no longer feels bound by an immutable, eternal law, the results can only be strife and discord, hatred and disunion, disorder and chaos."

Queen Victoria chartered the University of Laval in 1852, the year John Henry Newman published "The Idea of a University," which Halifax invoked as a prophecy for 1943: "Acutely aware of that peril to Western civilization which accompanied the rapid increase and consequent specialization of knowledge, he fore-saw that the human mind would be plunged in chaos if it was unhappily deprived of some general principle of interpretation. This, he insisted, theology alone could give. And he argued that theology, so far from restricting knowledge or limiting our hori-zon, was the true inspiration of all our learning. Now, with slow and halting steps, the world returns to the wisdom of Newman – that 'religious truth is not only a presentation, but a condition of general knowledge. . . .'"

Dr. Edvard Beneš was in Canada at the same time, lecturing on the importance of post-war accommodation with the Soviet Union. The exiled president of Czechoslovakia, with headquar-ters in London and residence in a country house in Buckinghamshire, had recently been in New York where he spoke in Carnegie Hall: "It was a cardinal mistake (after the last war) to imagine that we could devise a permanent peace settle-ment in Paris when no Russian representatives were invited to the peace table." Innocent in his own way about the Communists as Halifax had been in the late 1930s about the Nazis, Beneš certainly was no Communist himself. After the war, he became president of a coalition Czechoslovakian govern-ment, but refused to sign a Communist constitution in 1948 and died three months later, succeeded by his Communist prime minister, Clement Gottwald.

In the United States, money was collected for the relief of Poles in Russia. Out of an estimated million Polish children in the U.S.S.R., 40 percent had died, according to Msgr. Jozef

Gawlina, bishop of the Military Ordinariate of Poland with special responsibilities for Polish refugees. The Soviets maintained that everyone living in territory occupied by the Red Armies in 1939 became a Soviet national, and that preference in the distribution of foreign assistance should not be given to Poles.

On May 26 the Vatican radio crackled with indignation in German and French in response to the Nazi puppet Radio Paris, which had slandered the late Pope Pius XI three days before: "Achtung! Attention! On the evening of May 23rd Radio Paris broadcast an attack on the attitude of the Holy See at the present time . . . To this our reply is, briefly, that the attitude of the Catholic Church to National Socialism as a philosophy is known, in the first place, through the encyclical 'Mit Brennender Sorge.' All the world knows the facts about the fate of the Catholic Church in Germany. Radio Paris allegations therefore need no further refutation; we can only guess that they were made for propaganda purposes. All the same, it is impossible to see how that sort of thing can be useful, even as propaganda. One thing is certain: it was not the Vatican which declared this war, and it was not the Catholic Church in Germany which brought this, her fate, upon herself. All the world knows this." Surprisingly, on May 30, the Radio Paris spokesman, "Dr. Friedrich," apologized. He was Dr. Friedrich Sieburg, one-time Paris correspondent of the *Frankfurter Zeitung* and a protégé of Goebbels. "Dr. Friedrich" said that the transmission had been done by an "imposter" and that he had been surprised to hear it from his hospital bed: "Thanks to the perfect freedom of speech and expression which I am granted by Radio Paris, this talk, wrongly bearing my name, was broadcast by someone else, my illness preventing me from intervening."

The next day, the Vatican radio broadcast again in German a personal message Pope Pius XII had sent in October 1942 to the German bishops. The message anticipated the annual meeting of the bishops on June 5, the feast of St. Boniface, Apostle of Germany. The Pope had spent nearly half his Episcopal years in Germany and took this occasion to deplore the way "many people strive to do away with that ancient glory which hitherto we have so deeply admired, to destroy what the Christian religion gave Germany through so many centuries." The Pope expressed his gratitude to the German bishops who, with Rome, "are doing everything in their power to erect a bastion against those wretched people who harbour so hostile and unjustified an aversion to Christianity." The Pope invoked the early Christian martyrs as forerunners, and prayed that the bishops might be given a particular energy (Tatkraft) to fight the foe so that "the remotest times to come will give you thanks and will bless your memory in undying love." The words were blunt about the cost of discipleship. "Our profound solicitude is rightly due to the priests, Brothers and Sisters in professions, who are prepared rather to suffer the worst than to abandon the holy teaching of Christ. It is due to their saintly conduct that the Church in Germany shines in a new and marvelous splendour. We confess that this gives Us comfort and confidence, since the Lord is wont to grant His crown to the steadfast. You are all fighting for the glory of the Gospel, for which to die is Life, to live without which is living death."

Air raids in Germany took their toll in Mainz, Cologne and Lübeck. Severe damage was done to St. Hedwig's cathedral in Berlin, the early Gothic church of St. Stephen at Mainz, the tenth-century Minster at Essen with its frescoes and reliquaries, the thirteenth-century Marienkirche of Lübeck along with that city's cathedral and Petrikirche.

There was some confusion among the German propagandists who simultaneously banned the scientific works of the priest Copernicus as "of Polish origin" while claiming him as a German for the centennial commemoration of his death on May 24, 1543. Gauleiter Forster donated a statue of Copernicus to Thorn while Reichsminister Rust used the debt of Galileo the Italian to Copernicus the German as a metaphor for the Rome-Berlin Axis. In a speech at Königsberg, Rust said: "Germany today, the standard-bearer of the civilized nations of Europe in the struggle for life and freedom of her people and the values of a culture going back over three thousand years, regards Copernicus with sentiments of pride and indebtedness as one of the great ones who have embodied the German character and the German spirit most successfully. But the traitors to the life and civilization of Europe who, evil and false as never before in history, commit any act of murder and treason disguised in priest's garb and with prayers on their lips – these only remain true to themselves if they, the abettors of Katyn Wood, today celebrate Copernicus as 'the Pole.'"

May 27 saw the death in Spain at San Sebastian of the Marquis de Merry del Val, holder of the Grand Cross of the Victorian Order and brother of the late Cardinal Merry del Val, Pope St. Pius X's secretary of state. Born in London 79 years before, the Marquis had been Spanish ambassador to the Court of Saint James, his father having been secretary to the Spanish legation in London. He had resigned on the proclamation of the Spanish republic and was grieved at what he considered to be the failure of Britain and the United States to deplore the fall of the monarchy.

On May 24, Pope Pius XII received in farewell audience the German Ambassador to the Holy See, Dr. Carl-Ludwig Diego von Bergen. As the son of a German diplomat and a Spanish mother, he was born in Siam and early in his own diplomatic career had served in the German legation in Peking during the Boxer Rebellion. Outwardly a staunch Nazi, he had raised eyebrows at the obsequies for Pope Pius XI when, speaking as dean of the Vatican diplomatic corps by virtue of his seniority, he bid the cardinals to elect a Pope who would work with the Fascist governments to build "a new world upon the ruins of a past that in many things has no longer any reason to exist." But he was considered rather soft by Hitler and his retirement age, after 23 years in the Vatican, made it convenient to replace him with Baron Ernst von Weizacker. The new ambassador was a pragmatist who had opposed the invasion of Czechoslovakia because it would start a war that he did not think Germany could win. When the "Final Solution" was made known, he called it a "devilish campaign." From the Vatican, his correspondence to the home office in Berlin described Pius XII as overly-subtle, indecisive and disposed toward Germany, but one of his staff, Albrecht von Kessel, later said that this was a deliberate calculation to evoke sympathy for Germany among the Italians. Weizacker was convinced that Hitler intended to occupy the Vatican, which he thought would be disastrous, especially if the Pope were shot "fleeing while avoiding arrest." After the war, he remained in the Vatican as a guest of the Pope until 1946. In 1949 he was sentenced to seven years for war crimes, and later granted amnesty. Churchill believed him to have been anti-Nazi and called the conviction a travesty. One son, Carl, was an atomic physicist and philosopher, and a younger son, Richard, who had been a legal counsel to his father at the trial, became the first president of a united Germany, honored by many nations including Israel.

The 38-year-old missionary to the Norwegians, Father Hugo van der Vlugt, whose disappearance was announced in January, died in a German concentration camp. Forty-five years older, Msgr. Emanuel-Anatole-Raphael Chaptal de Chanteloup, auxiliary bishop of Paris, died on May 27, still wearing the star of David in protest against the persecution of the Jews.

24. Riots, Coups and Abdications

As in the month of June the Nazi racial policies would become more diabolic, climaxing with the installation of a third crematory in Birkenau by the end of the month. There was some irony in the contagion of race riots among some engaged in the war effort against the Axis. First came the so-called "Zoot Suit Riots" in Los Angeles, so named for the flamboyant clothing worn by youths enamored of "swing" music culture, especially Mexican immigrants. Riots began on June 3 when some 60 enlisted men from the Los Angeles Naval Reserve Armory began to beat up anyone fitting the racial profile. When Eleanor Roosevelt ventured a commentary on the Los Angeles chaos, the *Los Angeles Times* accused her of meddling and imputed Communist sympathies to her. On June 16, two died in race riots in Beaumont, Texas; another riot there followed on the 19th, leaving 21 dead, more than 200 wounded, and more than one hundred homes of black families looted. Shipbuilding for the Navy was impeded for months. In Detroit on June 20, the same day that the Germans rounded up Jews in Amsterdam for extermination, 35 were killed, 25 of them black, and 433 were wounded. It was a setback for the automobile industry under government contracts for the war effort, and Japanese propaganda shipped over flyers telling black citizens to turn against their government which was engaged in a "war between two races."

A military coup in Argentina by General Arturo Rawson and Colonel Juan Peron, first thought to be pro-Axis as they repudiated the neutrality policy of President Ramon Castillo, was just the opposite. Rawson was president for just three days but the new government was an opening for U.S. Under Secretary of

State, Sumner Welles, to assuage Latin American suspicions of "dollar diplomacy" by expressing respect for Catholic culture in the southern hemisphere. This followed the establishment of the Catholic Latin-American Institute with Bishop Edwin O'Hara of Kansas City as patron. Father Joseph Thorning, a missionary priest from Maryland, proclaimed that "no less than 80 per cent of the Argentinians, whether city dwellers or farmers, are hoping and praying with all the fervour of their Christian faith" for an Allied victory. These looked upon Bishop de Andrea, auxiliary for Buenos Aires, as their spokesman. An English language weekly, the *Southern Cross*, which was the journal of the Irish community in Buenos Aires, maintained what an English report called "an enthusiasm for the allied cause impermissible in their mother country. The paper said "There is no living Argentine so trusted and beloved as Bishop Miguel de Andrea. He is neither of the Left nor of the Right, yet both Rightists and Leftists put their confidence in him unreservedly when, as has so often happened, he has intervened unofficially and as a friend, to solve the angry questions which divide Labour from Capital." Argentina, with a large émigré German population and the last of the Latin American countries to support the Allies, was also home to the Catholic review *Orden Cristiano* promoting the social principles of Pope Leo XIII.

In France, a Jesuit journal, *Renouveaux*, was salvaging the integrity of French Catholicism from the temptations, under Vichy, to become what Jacques Maritain had recently called a "decoratively Christian State." The journal attacked the Vichy Government's exclusion of members of Catholic Action from civil and military posts. Rome had supported the resistance in frowning upon the participation of clerical participation in civic ceremonies orchestrated by the Vichy government. An unexpected response to the Church's stand against the occupiers was an increase in Mass attendance in French churches and pilgrimages, including an unprecedented number of pilgrims in Lourdes. By a stratagem cogent to those familiar with the ways of men, the reaction had its counter-reaction. The Vatican radio broadcast an account of the French government's policy to teach schoolboys how to blaspheme: "In the evening the boys (all about 14 or 15 years old) have to report to their leader, who encourages blasphemy by every means at his disposal, including money prizes. They 'examine their consciences,' and if they have failed to use the latest words that they have learnt, they must find an opportunity to use them before retiring."

During the increasing tension between Christian and anti-Christian pedagogies, the Church's material resources were evaporating. Seminaries were closing for lack of funds. Many priests were on the verge of starvation, with average resources of no more than 4,000 a year most. One egg was 20 francs and a chicken was 250 francs. A packet of twenty cigarettes was 120 francs, far beyond a priest's means, and so sometimes the faithful would place a few Gauloises cigarettes in the collection basket. Many priests were responsible for up to six parishes, reachable only by foot or bicycle. With all servants engaged in the army or other war efforts, the parish priest was also his own housekeeper, sexton and sacristan. One writer reported: "I have known one priest who has lived entirely on bread and olives; another who buys his bread only once so that so that it goes stale and he eats less . . . And I have before my eyes the pathetic story, at the age of 70, of a curé in the Basses-Alpes, who was found frozen to death in his lonely room in the winter. He had been in the habit of covering twenty kilometers on foot every Sunday, to visit six parishes."

On the feast of his patron St. Eugenius, June 2, which also was the start of the German assault on Sebastopol Krim, the Pope replied to the greetings of the College of Cardinals tendered by their doyen, Cardinal Granito Pignatelli di Belmonte. He spoke of "those who, because of their nationality or their descent, are pursued by mounting misfortune and increasing suffering. Sometimes, through no fault of their own, they are subjected to measures which threaten them with extermination." Of the small nations, "You do not expect Us to expound in detail all that We have attempted and undertaken to alleviate their sufferings . . .

Every single word in Our statements addressed to the competent authorities, and every one of Our public utterances, has had to be weighed and pondered by us with deep gravity, in the very interest of those who are suffering, so as not to render their position even more difficult and unbearable than before. . . ." And then, perhaps in response to the persistence of representatives of the Polish government in exile: "We wish to direct your compassion in a special manner to the Polish people, which, surrounded by powerful nations, is subjected to the blows of fate, and to the changing tides of the gigantic tragedy of war . . . We beseech the Queen of Heaven that this people, so cruelly tried, and those nations which with them have had to drain the bitter cup of this war, may have reserved for them a future in keeping with their legitimate aspirations and the magnitude of their sacrifices, in a Europe renewed on Christian foundation and within a body of nations free from the errors and waywardness of past and present times." Nine days later, Heinrich Himmler orders the liquidation of all Polish ghettos.

In June, the London press finally received a translation of the pastoral letter signed by the seven bishops of Slovakia for reading in all Slovak churches on March 21: "We demand that equal civil rights and State protection shall be accorded to every member of the State without distinction of origin or nationality. . . ." Protestant church leaders followed upon the Catholic bishops in their condemnation of forced labor: "There is a complete contradiction between the Gospel which is entrusted to the Church, and a conception of humanity which can be bought or seized at will, without consideration for the person, the conscience, or the most sacred feelings of the worker."

Msgr. George von Bayern, Protonotary Apostolic and a Canon of St. Peter's, died in Rome on May 31 at the age of 63 in the Villa San Francesco with the Franciscan Brothers of Waldbreitbach. He was the favorite grandson of the late Emperor Franz Joseph of Austria and, through his father, Prince Leopold, inherited the Stuart blood of the royal house of Bavaria, and also was heir to the crown of Greece. A champion boxer, he also served with distinction in the First World War on both fronts, and Palestine under General Ernst von Falenhayen, receiving the Iron Cross first and second class. His marriage in Vienna in 1912 to the Archduchess Isabelle of Austria was annulled by the Rota, after she deserted him on their honeymoon. Cardinal Franz Nagi had married them in the Schönbrunn Palace in 1912. He died, it is said, from tuberculosis, contracted while nursing patients in a Rome hospital. Money left by him paid for the new bronze doors of St. Peter's: the "Door of Death" by Giacomo Manzu and the "Door of the Sacraments" by Venanzo Crocetti. On June 7, the Pope received in audience Msgr. von Bayern's brother, Crown Prince Ruprecht of Bavaria. There was some speculation that his son, Albert, 38 years old, might be a figure of significance in the reconstruction of Germany at the end of the war. Among German monarchists, Prince Rupert had long been more popular than the Hohenzollerns. Two weeks earlier, the former Crown Prince of Saxony, Father Georg, S.J., drowned in Berlin. He had entered the Society of Jesus, relinquishing all claims to royal succession, in 1924. In 1918 he was engaged to Duchess Marie Amelia, daughter of the heir to the throne of Würtemberg. The wedding was cancelled with the end of the Saxon monarchy and his desire to enter Holy Orders. Like the fiancée of Msgr. von Bayern, the Duchess never married. In Berlin, he had been a clandestine protector of Jews, and a foe of the Nazis, though his death by drowning was ruled the result of a heart attack. In his diary, found on the lakeshore, he had written: "Vado ad Patrem." – "I go to the Father."

Having been informed that the Nazi "Agricultural Front" was taking control of all Catholic Agricultural Schools, the Dutch bishops instructed parents immediately to remove their children from those schools.

His Eminence Achille Cardinal Lienart of Lille, where he was bishop for forty years beginning in 1928, continued to irritate the Nazis. Although he had initially been a supporter of Pétain, he was an uncompromising foe of the National Socialists. He was a particular target for the Paris journal "Au Pilori," which was an anti-Semitic journal funded with German money all through the war at 43 rue Monceau in the 8th Arrondissement. "He is anti-national, and protects certain Freemasons of high rank. . . . He is a saboteur of French resurrection; his last sermon proves this. He is 1,000 percent (sic) Anglophile, and just as much anti-collaborationist." *Le Pays Rél*, a paper in the same vein as *Au Pilori*, took up its case against the nuns at Namur, who "Listen tenderly to their pupils, duly trained, singing the praise of murderers and expressing the hope that the dear heroes of the R.A.F. will burn and devastate our country."

25. Ascalon

The Avro York LV 633 "Ascalon" was an air transport developed in 1942, somewhat bulky in appearance with wings mounted high in the fuselage. It was Churchill's favorite flight model, with enough space for a conference room. The name "Ascalon" was the traditional name for the lance used by St. George to slay the dragon, and in turn it was taken from the Israeli coastal city of Ashkelon for its associations with the First Crusade. At the beginning of June in 1943, King George VI used it for his visit to the troops in North Africa, principally to Montgomery and the Eighth Army. He was welcomed as well by Eisenhower and Patton. Following the victory at El Alamein, Montgomery did not discourage exuberant press comparisons of him with the Duke of Wellington. After the king's trip, which took him to Algiers and Tripoli and then on to Malta where he was greeted by long lines of cheering troops, His Majesty declared the visit a success and commented how relieved he was to see that Montgomery was not after his job. The cautious jubilation of the royal visit was a stark contrast to the scene exactly one year before, when the Afrika Korps recaptured Tobruk and the British retreated into Egypt, where Rommel had even captured Marsa Matruh, only 140 miles from Alexandria, and the British prepared for their "final stand" at El Alamein.

The "Ascalon" was a modest craft, compared with the first jet-propulsion bomber, the Arado Ar 234, first tested by the Germans on June 15. The Allies, for all their advances, had nothing like it. But the air war against the Japanese was promising, and on June 16, over Guadalcanal, the United States forces repulsed an attack, destroying 107 Japanese airplanes, and missing only 13.

Thoughts were turning to the rebirth of a free French Army. Long memories of the French defeat in 1870, and experience of a restless military that tried to revive Napoleonic imperialism, had inclined Clemenceau in 1881 to envision a national militia instead of a professional army. But so long as there was a German army, that was delusional, and in the Third Republic the French army flourished. But the "affaire Dreyfus," which had rallied many integrist Catholics against an innocent Jew, had sown the seeds for divisions in the army right up to the Second World War. Any political conservative, and certainly any conservative Catholic even including Marshal Foch, was suspect in the military establishment until the emergency of the First World War, which had erased the old stereotypes. With the decline of Vichy fortunes in 1943, many hoped that a similar healing and reunion of French parties might happen under the leadership of General Giraud backed by General Eisenhower.

Himmler gave orders on June 12 to destroy all Polish ghettoes and transport those in them to death camps. On June 13, German aircraft killed seventy-four Allied troops in a raid over Britain. The blitz still lived. On that day, too, Stalin launched a vast Soviet propaganda project, using the film director Mikhail Slutsky and 240 cameras to film scenes of fighting on the Russian front. It was Whitsunday in England, the latest possible date for Pentecost to fall on the liturgical calendar. It will not happen again until 2038. Pope Pius XII chose that day to address 26,000 working men who had gone on pilgrimage to Rome from the farthest reaches of Italy despite the difficult circumstances of the war closing in from the south. The British had invaded Pantelleria, an island south of Sicily, on the 11th. The Pope, mentioning neither Nazis nor Communists by name, told the workers: "The Church, Guardian and Teacher of Truth, in asserting and defending courageously the rights of the working classes on various occasions, and in combating error, has had to raise Her voice against letting oneself be deluded by the mirage of pernicious and fatuous theories and visions of future well-being, and against the deceptive enticements and attractions of false prophets of social prosperity who call evil good and good evil. . . . Social revolution claims to give power into the hands of the working class – empty words, mirages incapable of realization. In fact we see that the working class remains bound, choked and tied to the force of State Capitalism, which restrains and subjects all, not only the family but even the conscience, and transforms the workers into a gigantic labour machine. Like the other social systems and orders which it claims to fight, it classifies, regulates and transforms all into a brutal war machine which demands not only blood and health, but also the wealth and prosperity of a people."

On the same feast, the Vatican wireless seemed to reiterate some of the themes of Cardinal Faulhaber's ordination jubilee pastoral letter on August 1, 1942, and spoke of Pentecost as "specifically the feast of the priesthood. Let us pray, therefore, for many and good priests. This is doubly necessary in our times. In these days the dangers for the kingdom of God are great, and great are the sufferings of priests. In many regions a veritable persecution of priests is raging. Priests are persecuted, deported, maltreated. Many die as a result of the sufferings inflicted on them . . . In these attacks, celibacy, which is precisely what makes the priest of the Western Church a true and self-sacrificing servant in the vineyard of the Lord, is made a special butt; it is said to be meaningless, and opposed to the growth of the nationhood . . . Parents, protect your children; protect them from the dangers threatening their faith. Teach them true ideas about priests and priesthood. Help them to reject with contempt all false slogans which are bandied about today, to be steadfast in the midst of an age which knows no better than to despise and persecute everything supernatural and all true values."

In the second week of June, the full text of the Joint Pastoral Letter of the Dutch hierarchy, read in all the churches of the Netherlands on May 16, was finally translated for the English press. "A world outlook which is diametrically opposed to Christianity has been forced upon our people these last three years. In every sphere Nazism attempts to extend its influence and take control. Although Nazism remains the powerful master of the situation here, the spiritual power of resistance of the overwhelming majority of the Netherlands people is unbroken. This fills us with great consolations and faith in the future. Despite all suppression of those differently minded and the bait of various material advantages, the Netherlands people will never become Nazi if we remain but loyal to our ancestral faith . . . the only power that can fight Communism is not Nazism, but Christianity. For 'nobody may lay another foundation than that laid, which is Christ.'"

The Reichskommissar in the Netherlands, Arthur Seyss-Inquart, was a lapsed Catholic totally devoted to National Socialism and a confidant of Hitler. His brother Richard had been a ordained a Catholic priest but abandoned the priesthood to marry. He became a prison official in Ostmark. Seyss-Inquart responded to the bishops: "The best proof of the magnanimous freedom which we grant is the fact that such a Pastoral Letter can be read without hindrance. Comrades, in our midst you cannot create martyrs! Certainly it is true that there are priests in prison. I have every single dossier brought before me. These men, however, are very real offenders. They have committed offences; they have either slandered the Reich or National Socialism or the Führer in a fashion which one simply cannot tolerate, or they have committed acts of espionage or helped the enemy. . . ."

At the beginning of June, the Dutch bishops replied to Reichskommisar Seyss-Inquart with the unprecedented joint signatures of leaders of all eight Protestant bodies in the land: the Dutch Reformed, three Calvinist bodies, two Lutheran Evangelical, the Remonstrants and the Mennonites, in protest against the government policy of sterilizing couples in mixed marriages: "As things are, you are entrusted with the maintenance of order and law in the country. You are entrusted with this not only by the Führer of the German Reich, but also through the inscrutable dispensation of God, Whom the Church proclaims on earth. To you apply, exactly as to all other men, and to you especially because you happen to be placed in this high office, the Commandments of this Lord and Judge of the entire earth. . . .We have no illusions. We are well aware that we can hardly expect your Excellency to heed the voice of the Church, that is the voice of the Gospel, that is the voice of God. But what we cannot hope for as a human achievement, we dare to hope for in our Faith in Christ. The living God has power to convert and to change your Excellency's heart. For that, too, we pray to God for the good of your Excellency and our suffering people." Seyss-Inquart was sentenced to death at the Nuremburg trials, and was hanged on October 16, 1946, having asked to return to the Church and making his confession to the prison chaplain.

Given censorship in occupied Paris, reliable information came to the Allies through complicated and slow routes. It was the American Office of War Information that received word in the first days of June, but only reported in August, that the Superior-General of the Sisters of St. Paul in Paris, along with two other religious sisters of the same order, had been arrested by the Gestapo "in an attempt to learn the location of a French Sister of Charity who is said to have engineered the liberation of many French military prisoners." The immediate fate of the prisoners was unknown, though they brought to mind some other Sisters of Charity: Odile Baumgarten and Marie-Anne Vaillot shot by a firing squad in the French Revolution in 1794 for having refused to take an oath of obedience to the new government's fabricated Constitutional Church, and ten other Sisters of Charity who had left France as missionaries to China, martyred after macabre tortures in T'ien-tsin in 1870.

26. Life Worthy of Living

June 1943 marked the start of the third year of war between Germany and Russia, the latter still fighting with remarkable energy in "The Great Patriotic War" in spite of, or perhaps inspired by, the largest numbers of casualties in the history of warfare. Germany no longer was guided by a hunger for "lebensraum" in Ukraine and the Russian frontier districts. An esoteric symbol of this revised strategy was the Russian defector, General Andrey Andreyovich Vlassov. The Communist Party, which he joined in 1930, eventually gave him the Order of Lenin and the Red Banner. Chiang Kai-shek used him as a military advisor, bestowing on him the Order of the Golden Dragon, and then he commanded the Fourth Mechanized Soviet Army Corps at Lwow when the Germans invaded, held several commands in Ukraine, and then was given command of guerrillas behind the German lines for six months before being taken prisoner on the Volkhov front in 1942. Declaring himself an anti-Stalinist, he soon embraced National Socialism at least to the degree that it might help him form a Russian Liberation Army. To this end, the Germans helped him drop millions of his "Smolensk Proclamation" from aircraft over Russian troops. By May 1943, the Russian Liberation Army, an official entity only when Himmler overcame Hitler's reservations about it in 1944, numbered 150,000 men, according to the *Aftonbladet*, a pro-German newspaper in Sweden.

This hybrid army included numbers of White Russians who had settled in Germany after the Russian Revolution. At the end of the war, on the twelfth of May, 1945, an American escort which had held Vlassov prisoner offered no resistance to his capture by a Russian contingent. Imprisoned and tortured in the Lubyanka prison in Moscow, he finally was hanged on August 1, 1946. However mixed his motives were, the Russian Federation eventually de-classified him as a traitor. There even is a monument to the general – who had studied for the priesthood in a Russian seminary before the Revolution – in the Novo Deveevo Russian Orthodox convent in Nanuet, New York, where special prayers are offered on the anniversary of his assassination.

The Vlassov saga was a sign that the Germans had concluded that they could not defeat the Russians and were aiming at a stalemate. The *Aftonbladet* concluded from Hitler's gesture of granting a private meeting with Vlassov that the Führer had decided "to seek collaboration among the occupied eastern countries. The propaganda began by arguing that there was no reason why the German and Slav brethren should not live peacefully side by side. England started the war, so Stalin is actually a prisoner of the British plutocrats, and therefore it is the duty of every decent Slav to fight together with the Germans until Stalin is overthrown and peace is secured."

In the United States, the Japanese war was a specter as grave as the hostilities in Europe, and many eyes were looking on Stalinism as a problem that would outrun Nazism. Forty-eight-year-old Msgr. Fulton J. Sheen of the Catholic University of America was already so well-known a speaker and Catholic apologist that he had been invited in April 1943 to speak in Montreal on Nazism as a pseudo-religion challenging Christianity. He switched the focus to Stalinism, quoting what he claimed was a secret report of the Third International Congress in Mexico in 1941: "This war is but an accident. The end of it is to be used for fostering revolution. The immediate foe is Nazi Germany, but it must never be forgotten that there are two great capitalist regimes to be overthrown – America and Britain. Directives were given the delegates. Russia must be everywhere portrayed as the saviour of democracy and her right established to dictate, and dictate alone, the condition of the post-war world.

Everyone who opposes Communism is to be labeled Fascist, whether he be a Conservative, Monarchist, Liberal, or anything else."

In a very different and highly esoteric vein were the ponderous, if not pretentious, musings of Baron Giulio Cesare Andrea Evola, who wrote a regular cultural column, "Panorama," in Farinacci's *Regime Fascista*. Evola was hard to categorize philosophically, and he never joined the National Fascist Party despite a close association with Mussolini. It is doubtful that the Duce knew what to make of Evola's "radical traditionalism" which was mixed up with Vajcayantist Tantric Yoga and Tibetan Lamaism, and it is clear that Evola was too much of an intellectual aesthete to think of institutionalized Fascism as anything but structuralized vulgarity. As one of his baroque flights of fancy, he identified his racial philosophy with the Germano-imperialism of the mediaeval Ghibbelines opposed to the pro-Papal Guelphs. In his parallel universe, he espied the Catholic Church of Pius XII, in its inhospitality to Fascism, as a "neo-Guelph" corruption of European idealism, manipulated by Freemasons and democrats. "The neo-Guelphs speak of Christ, of Rome, of Roman universality, and so on. But the effective cement of their common front is composed of the following elements: They will not listen to any talk about race; they view the anti-Jewish struggle as a retrogression into obscurantism; they cherish anti-German sentiments; they look upon the Axis as an error, and consider any rapprochement with Germany as a betrayal of the German tradition. . . . As the Duce himself has said, if 'Fascist' and 'Catholic' can exist at the same time, it is the term 'Fascist' which must be the most in evidence, and must set the standard for those elements of Catholicism which may be accepted and assimilated on the ethical and political plane."

In London, *The Tablet* described Georges Suarez of the Paris *Aujourd'hui* as "among the chief collaborating haters of the Church. Particularly disgusted by Cardinal Suhard's resistance to compulsory labor conscription, Suarez wrote that "the higher clergy had been turned into instruments of Stalinist and

Gaulliste propaganda in our country." Suarez called those clergy opposed to the Nazi occupiers "cassocked demagogues."

In mid-June, Archbishop Francis J. Spellman was on one of his mysterious international voyages. By the third week, he was in Uganda. His visit to the Polish Army in the Middle East got wide praise in the Polish-American press. The *Nowiny Polskie* of Milwaukee hailed him and the Boston *Kuyier Codzienny* expected that Spellman's visit would be significant for post-war reconstruction.

On the 14th of June, the United States VIII Corps arrived in the European theater. On the 16th, a vast Soviet offensive took back Kalinin. The next day marked the death of the legendary Dominican friar, Father Vincent McNabb. His disquisitions on the Faith in Hyde Park and his austere practice of poverty, even to the point of eccentricity in more comfortable witnesses, made him a prime figure in the Catholic life of London, but one described as flitting back and forth between the twentieth century and the thirteenth. Msgr. Ronald Knox, thinking McNabb possibly a saint, noticed "a kind of light about his presence." G. K. Chesterton had once said ". . . he is one of the few great men I have known in my life . . . he is great in many ways, mentally and morally and mystically and practically . . . nobody who ever met or saw or heard Father McNabb has ever forgotten him." Seven years before, on June 14, Father McNabb attended Chesterton on his deathbed and chanted the "Salve Regina" hymn precious to the Dominicans, one of whom, St. Thomas Aquinas, had been the subject of Chesterton's biography, "The Dumb Ox." Under war rationing and restrictions on transportation, Hilaire Belloc traveled from Sussex to London for his Requiem. In the tumultuous war years, Father McNabb pushed with a particular urgency for a memorial to St. Thomas More in the Law Courts, as a reminder of the integrity of the law in a lawless world.

Perhaps worn down by the experience of recent years, the publishers of the "International Who's Who" placed an advisory at the beginning of their new edition: "American readers are asked to note that the term 'politician' is used in the English sense, as meaning 'one engaged in politics,' and has no derogatory application." St. Thomas More would have understood the clarification.

A new book by the Oxford don, C. S. Lewis, was published under the title "Christian Behaviour." It consisted of radio broadcasts he had given on Christian ethics. A 39-year-old Robert Speaight reviewed it in *The Tablet*. He had converted to Roman Catholicism and, as an actor, distinguished himself in the role of *Becket* in the first production of T. S. Eliot's *Murder in the Cathedral*. Speaight was not an enthusiast of Lewis, and welcomed the new book on the heels of *The Screwtape Letters* which, despite its "acrid brilliance" bespoke "a dualism which at least one reader reader found unappealing." Speaight welcomed Lewis's newly found "sane Christian humanism" which seemed only fledgling in earlier works and commented: "The Christian teaching on purity is generally unpopular and generally unpracticed; and so – though fewer will admit it – is the Christian teaching on forgiveness and humility. How many people who talk glibly about Christian principles really believe that chastity or lowliness of heart are admirable things?"

General Eisenhower was named head of "Overlord," the projected invasion of Normandy. Then on June 29, the Japanese gave control of the Andaman Islands to Hukumate Azad Hind, a "Provisional Government of Free India" established in Singapore in 1943. It was opposed to British rule in India and functioned virtually as a puppet state of Japan, not recognized as a diplomatic entity by the Allies or Vichy France. Azad Hind had less influence on the next generation than the encyclical "Mystici Corporis" published on the same June 29th. The winds of war detracted attention from it at the time, but it influenced the Second Vatican Council and much conversation about human rights even in the secular sphere.

By teaching the supernatural and incarnational realities of the Church, Pope Pius XII rejected materialistic reductions of the Church to merely a humanitarian and social organization.

Equally, the Pope rejected a falsely pious impression of the Church as nothing more than an association of individuals engaged in a personal experience of God with no social consequences. Much of the encyclical's language was obviously, save to the most obtuse, a commentary on unreal social engineering of the Nazis. Of racial mythology and eugenics, the Pope said: "And first of all let us imitate the breadth of His love. For the Church, the Bride of Christ, is one; and yet so vast is the love of the divine Spouse that it embraces in His Bride the whole human race without exception. Our Saviour shed His Blood precisely in order that He might reconcile men to God through the Cross, and might constrain them to unite in one body, however widely they may differ in nationality and race. True love of the Church, therefore, requires not only that we should be mutually solicitous one for another as members and sharing in their suffering but likewise that we should recognize in other men, although they are not yet joined to us in the body of the Church, our brothers in Christ according to the flesh, called, together with us, to the same eternal salvation."

As for brutal extermination of "life unworthy of life" ("Lebensunwertes Leben") as the Nazis had refrained in earlier genetic theory: "Conscious of the obligations of Our high office We deem it necessary to reiterate this grave statement today, when to Our profound grief We see at times the deformed, the insane, and those suffering from hereditary disease deprived of their lives, as though they were a useless burden to Society; and this procedure is hailed by some as a manifestation of human progress, and as something that is entirely in accordance with the common good. Yet who that is possessed of sound judgment does not recognize that this not only violates the natural and the divine law written in the heart of every man, but that it outrages the noblest instincts of humanity? The blood of these unfortunate victims who are all the dearer to our Redeemer because they are deserving of greater pity, 'cries to God from the earth.'"

So the warring went on, as it would for more than two years, and the philosophical commentaries mixed with political plans made sense only by looking at Jesus being crucified in those days. In the spiritual combat of World War II, the fighters had to be fed and sheltered as Jesus did when he fed the multitudes before he preached. He spoke in every wartime appeal for assistance to those who were fighting. Christ, engaged on the palisades and frontiers of each battle, would have understood, and perhaps inspired, advertisements in the daily papers such as this one in London: "The word 'retreat' is not one with acceptable associations for soldiers, but nearly 1,000 of them, British, American and Dominion, have attended the week-end retreats for Service men that are held at Campion House, Osterley, and they are wearing out the house's limited supply of sheets. Despite careful patching, the preset stock is in urgent need of replenishment. Any number of sheets of any size or colour or kind (but preferably stout and of single size) will be gratefully received."

Sheets were sent and the war was won, but there is no end to such a war, for it began in Eden and will contend until the world itself returns to the eternity from which it was made.

Index of Names